STECK-VAUGHN

TABE®
Fundamentals

Focus on Skills

Applied Math

LEVEL M

2nd Edition

Steck Vaughn™

HOUGHTON MIFFLIN HARCOURT
Supplemental Publishers

www.SteckVaughn.com
800-531-5015

Reviewers

Victor Gathers
Regional Coordinator of Adult Services
New York City Department of Education
Brooklyn Adult Learning Center
Brooklyn, New York

Brannon Lentz
Assistant Director of Adult Education/Skills Training
Northwest Shoals Community College
Muscle Shoals, Alabama

Jean Pierre-Pipkin, Ed.D.
Director of Beaumont I.S.D. Adult Education
Cooperative Consortium
Beaumont, Texas

ISBN-13: 978-1-4190-5354-2
ISBN-10:   1-4190-5354-X

Contents

To the Learner

Congratulations on your decision to study for the TABE! You are taking an important step in your educational career. This book will help you do your best on the TABE. You'll also find hints and strategies that will help you prepare for test day. Practice these skills—your success lies in your hands.

What Is the TABE?

TABE stands for the Tests of Adult Basic Education. These paper-and-pencil tests, published by McGraw-Hill, measure your progress on basic skills. There are five tests in all: Reading, Mathematics Computation, Applied Mathematics, Language, and Spelling.

TABE Levels M, D, and A

Test	Number of Items	Suggested Working Time (in minutes)
1 Reading	50	50
2 Mathematics Computation	25	15
3 Applied Mathematics	50	50
4 Language	55	39
5 Spelling	20	10

Test 1 Reading

This test measures basic reading skills. The main concepts covered by this test are word meaning, critical thinking, and understanding basic information.

Many things on this test will look familiar to you. They include documents and forms necessary to your everyday life, such as directions, bank statements, maps, and consumer labels. The test also includes items that measure your ability to find and use information from a dictionary, table of contents, or library computer display. The TABE also tests a learner's understanding of fiction and nonfiction passages.

Test 2 Mathematics Computation

Test 2 covers adding, subtracting, multiplying, and dividing. On the test you must use these skills with whole numbers, fractions, decimals, integers, and percents.

The skills covered in the Mathematics Computation test are the same skills you use daily to balance your checkbook, double a recipe, or fix your car.

Test 3 Applied Mathematics

The Applied Mathematics test links mathematical ideas to real-world situations. Many things you do every day require basic math. Making budgets, cooking, and doing your taxes all take math. The test also covers pre-algebra, algebra, and geometry. Adults need to use all these skills.

Some questions will relate to one theme. For example, auto repairs could be the subject and the question could focus on the repair schedule. You may be told when a car was last repaired and how often it needs to be repaired. You might have to predict the next maintenance date.

Many of the items will not require you to use a specific strategy or formula to get the correct answer. Instead this test challenges you to use your own problem-solving strategies to answer the question.

Test 4 Language

The Language test asks you to analyze different types of writing. Examples are business letters, resumes, job reports, and essays. For each task, you have to show you understand good writing skills.

The questions fit adult interests and concerns. Some questions ask you to think about what is wrong in the written material. In other cases, you will correct sentences and paragraphs.

Test 5 Spelling

In everyday life, you need to spell correctly, especially in the workplace. The spelling words on this test are words that many people misspell and words that are commonly used in adult writing.

How to Use *TABE Fundamentals*

Test-Taking Tips

1. Read the directions very carefully. Make sure you read through them word for word. If you are not sure what the question says, ask the person giving the test to explain it to you.

2. Read each question carefully. Make sure you know what it means and what you have to do.

3. Read all of the answers carefully, even if you think you know the answer.

4. Make sure that the reading supports your answer. Don't answer without checking the reading. Don't rely only on outside knowledge.

5. Answer all of the questions. If you can't find the right answer, rule out the answers that you know are wrong. Then try to figure out the right answer. If you still don't know, make your best guess.

6. If you can't figure out the answer, put a light mark by the question and come back to it later. Erase your marks before you finish.

7. Don't change an answer unless you are sure your first answer is wrong. Usually your first idea is the correct answer.

8. If you get nervous, stop for a while. Take a few breaths and relax. Then start working again.

How to Use *TABE Fundamentals*

Step-by-Step Instruction In Levels M and D, each lesson starts with step-by-step instruction on a skill. The instruction contains examples and then a test example with feedback. This instruction is followed by practice questions. Work all of the questions in the lesson's practice and then check your work in the Answers and Explanations in the back of the book.

The Level A books contain practice for each skill covered on the TABE. Work all of the practice questions and then check your work in the Answers and Explanations in the back of the book.

Reviews The lessons in Levels M and D are grouped by a TABE Objective. At the end of each TABE Objective, there is a Review. Use these Reviews to find out if you need to review any of the lessons before continuing.

Performance Assessment At the end of every book, there is a special section called the Performance Assessment. This section is similar to the TABE test. It has the same number and type of questions. This assessment will give you an idea of what the real test is like.

Answer Sheet At the back of the book is a practice bubble-in answer sheet. Practice bubbling in your answers. Fill in the answer sheet carefully. For each answer, mark only one numbered space on the answer sheet. Mark the space beside the number that corresponds to the question. Mark only one answer per question. On the real TABE, if you have more than one answer per question, they will be scored as incorrect. Be sure to erase any stray marks.

Strategies and Hints Pay careful attention to the TABE Strategies and Hints throughout this book. Strategies are test-taking tips that help you do better on the test. Hints give you extra information about a skill.

Setting Goals

On the following page is a form to help you set your goals. Setting goals will help you get more from your work in this book.

Section 1. Why do you want to do well on the TABE? Take some time now to set your short-term and long-term goals on page 3.

Section 2. Making a schedule is one way to set priorities. Deadlines will help you stay focused on the steps you need to take to reach your goals.

Section 3. Your goals may change over time. This is natural. After a month, for example, check the progress you've made. Do you need to add new goals or make any changes to the ones you have? Checking your progress on a regular basis helps you reach your goals.

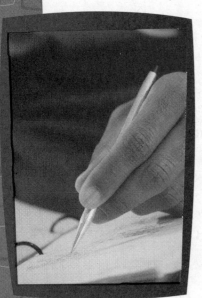

For more information on setting goals, see Steck-Vaughn's *Start Smart Goal Setting Strategies.*

1. Set Your Goals

What is your long-term goal for using this book?

_____
_____
_____

Complete these areas to identify the smaller steps to take to reach your long-term goal.

Content area	What I Know	What I Want to Learn
Reading	_____	_____
Language	_____	_____
Spelling	_____	_____
Math	_____	_____
Other	_____	_____

2. Make a Schedule

Set some deadlines for yourself.

> For a 20-week planning calendar, see Steck-Vaughn's *Start Smart Planner.*

Goals	Begin Date	End Date
_____	_____	_____
_____	_____	_____
_____	_____	_____
_____	_____	_____

3. Celebrate Your Success

Note the progress you've made. If you made changes in your goals, record them here.

_____
_____
_____
_____

To the Instructor

About TABE

The Tests of Adult Basic Education are designed to meet the needs of adult learners in ABE programs. Written and designed to be relevant to adult learners' lives and interests, this material focuses on the life, job, academic, and problem-solving skills that the typical adult needs.

Because of the increasing importance of thinking skills in any curriculum, *TABE Fundamentals* focuses on critical thinking throughout each TABE Objective.

The TABE identifies the following thinking processes as essential to learning and achieving goals in daily life:

- ✦ Gather Information
- ✦ Organize Information
- ✦ Analyze Information
- ✦ Generate Ideas
- ✦ Synthesize Elements
- ✦ Evaluate Outcomes

Test 1 Reading

The TABE measures an adult's ability to understand home, workplace, and academic texts. The ability to construct meaning from prose and visual information is also covered through reading and analyzing diagrams, maps, charts, forms, and consumer materials.

Test 2 Mathematics Computation

This test covers whole numbers, decimals, fractions, integers, percents, and algebraic expressions. Skills are carefully targeted to the appropriate level of difficulty.

Test 3 Applied Mathematics

This test emphasizes problem-solving and critical-thinking skills, with a focus on the life-skill applications of mathematics. Estimation and pattern-recognition skills also are important on this test.

Test 4 Language

The Language test focuses on writing and effective communication. Students examine writing samples that need revision, with complete-sentence and paragraph contexts for the various items. The test emphasizes editing, proofreading, and other key skills. The context of the questions are real-life settings appropriate to adults.

Test 5 Spelling

This test focuses on the words learners most typically misspell. In this way, the test identifies the spelling skills learners most need in order to communicate effectively. Items typically present high-frequency words in short sentences.

Uses of the TABE

There are three basic uses of the TABE:

Instructional

From an instructional point of view, the TABE allows instructors to assess students' entry levels as they begin an adult program. The TABE also allows instructors to diagnose learners' strengths and weaknesses in order to determine appropriate areas to focus instruction. Finally the TABE allows instructors and institutions to monitor learners' progress.

Administrative

The TABE allows institutions to assess classes in general and measure the effectiveness of instruction and whether learners are making progress.

Governmental

The TABE provides a means of assessing a school's or program's effectiveness.

The National Reporting System (NRS) and the TABE

Adult education and literacy programs are federally funded and thus accountable to the federal government. The National Reporting System monitors adult education. Developed with the help of adult educators, the NRS sets the reporting requirements for adult education programs around the country. The information collected by the NRS is used to assess the effectiveness of adult education programs and make necessary improvements.

A key measure defined by the NRS is educational gain, which is an assessment of the improvement in learners' reading, writing, speaking, listening, and other skills during their instruction. Programs assess educational gain at every stage of instruction.

NRS Functioning Level	Grade Level	TABE (7/8 and 9/10) scale scores
Beginning ABE Literacy	0–1.9	Reading . . . . 367 and below Total Math . . . . 313 and below Language . . . . . 392 and below
Beginning Basic Education	2–3.9	Reading . . . . 368–460 Total Math . . . . 314–441 Language 393–490
Low Intermediate Basic Education	4–5.9	Reading . . . . 461–517 Total Math . . . . 442–505 Language 491–523
High Intermediate Basic Education	6–8.9	Reading . . . . 518–566 Total Math . . . . 506–565 Language 524–559
Low Adult Secondary Education	9–10.9	Reading . . . . 567–595 Total Math . . . . 566–594 Language 560–585

According to the NRS guidelines, states select the method of assessment appropriate for their needs. States can assess educational gain either through standardized tests or through performance-based assessment. Among the standardized tests typically used under NRS guidelines is the TABE, which meets the NRS standards both for administrative procedures and for scoring.

The three main methods used by the NRS to collect data are the following:

1. **Direct program reporting,** from the moment of student enrollment
2. **Local follow-up surveys,** involving learners' employment or academic goals
3. **Data matching,** or sharing data among agencies serving the same clients so that outcomes unique to each program can be identified.

Two of the major goals of the NRS are academic achievement and workplace readiness. Educational gain is a means to reaching these goals. As learners progress through the adult education curriculum, the progress they make should help them either obtain or keep employment or obtain a diploma, whether at the secondary school level or higher. The TABE is flexible enough to meet both the academic and workplace goals set forth by the NRS.

Using *TABE Fundamentals*

Adult Basic Education Placement

From the outset, the TABE allows effective placement of learners. You can use the *TABE Fundamentals* series to support instruction of those skills where help is needed.

High School Equivalency

Placement often involves predicting learners' success on the GED, the high school equivalency exam. Each level of *TABE Fundamentals* covers Reading, Language, Spelling, Applied and Computational Math to allow learners to focus their attention where it is needed.

Assessing Progress

Each TABE skill is covered in a lesson. These lessons are grouped by TABE Objective. At the end of each TABE Objective, there is a Review. Use these Reviews to find out if the learners need to review any of the skills before continuing.

At the end of the book, there is a special section called the Performance Assessment. This section is similar to the TABE test. It has the same number and type of questions. You can use the Performance Assessment as a timed pretest or posttest with your learners, or as a more general review for the actual TABE.

Steck-Vaughn's *TABE Fundamentals* Program at a Glance

The charts on the following page provide a quick overview of the elements of Steck-Vaughn's *TABE Fundamentals* series. Use this chart to match the TABE objectives with the skill areas for each level. This chart will come in handy whenever you need to find which objectives fit the specific skill areas you need to cover.

Steck-Vaughn's *TABE Fundamentals* Program at a Glance

TABE OBJECTIVE

	Level M		Level D		Level A
	Reading	Language and Spelling	Reading	Language and Spelling	Reading, Language, and Spelling
Reading					
Interpret Graphic Information	✦		✦		✦
Words in Context	✦		✦		✦
Recall Information	✦		✦		✦
Construct Meaning	✦		✦		✦
Evaluate/Extend Meaning	✦		✦		✦
Language					
Usage		✦		✦	✦
Sentence Formation		✦		✦	✦
Paragraph Development		✦		✦	✦
Punctuation and Capitalization		✦		✦	✦
Writing Convention		✦		✦	✦
Spelling					
Vowel		✦		✦	✦
Consonant		✦		✦	✦
Structural Unit		✦		✦	✦

	Level M		Level D		Level A
	Math Computation	Applied Math	Math Computation	Applied Math	Computational and Applied Math
Mathematics Computation					
Addition of Whole Numbers	✦				
Subtraction of Whole Numbers	✦				
Multiplication of Whole Numbers	✦		✦		
Division of Whole Numbers	✦		✦		
Decimals	✦		✦		✦
Fractions	✦		✦		✦
Integers			✦		✦
Percents			✦		✦
Orders of Operation			✦		✦
Applied Mathematics					
Number and Number Operations		✦		✦	✦
Computation in Context		✦		✦	✦
Estimation		✦		✦	✦
Measurement		✦		✦	✦
Geometry and Spatial Sense		✦		✦	✦
Data Analysis		✦		✦	✦
Statistics and Probability		✦		✦	✦
Patterns, Functions, Algebra		✦		✦	✦
Problem Solving and Reasoning		✦		✦	✦

Lesson 1   Place Value

Which amount would you rather win in a raffle, $25 or $52? You would choose $52 because you know it has the greater value. The value of the digits 5 and 2 depend on their place in the number.

On the TABE you will determine the value of a digit based on its place value.

Example **Use a place value chart to find the value of a number. The cost of an economy car is $13,297. What is the value of the digit 3?**

Step 1. Write each digit of 13,297 in the correct place in the place value chart. The chart shows the value of each digit in the number.

	ten thousands 10,000s	thousands 1,000s	hundreds 100s	tens 10s	ones 1s
cost of an economy car	1	3	2	9	7

Step 2. Use the place value chart to determine the value of each digit.

The 1 is in the ten thousands place.	Its value is 1 ten thousand, or 1 × 10,000.
The 3 is in the thousands place.	Its value is 3 thousands, or 3 × 1,000.
The 2 is in the hundreds place.	Its value is 2 hundreds, or 2 × 100.
The 9 is in the tens place.	Its value is 9 tens, or 9 × 10.
The 7 is in the ones place.	Its value is 7 ones, or 7 × 1.

The value of the digit 3 in $13,297 is 3,000.

Test Example

Read the question. Circle the answer.

1   What does the 4 in 21,469 mean?

   A   4

   B   40

   C   400

   D   4,000

Hint

The value of each digit in a number decreases as you move to the right.

1   C   400 In the number 21,469, the 4 appears in the hundreds place. The 4 stands for 4 x 100, or 400. Option A shows the 4 in the ones place. Option B shows the 4 in the tens place. Option D shows the 4 in the thousands place.

Read the questions. Circle the answers.

1 What does the 7 in 17,812 mean?

A   70

B   700

C   7,000

D   70,000

2 What does the 1 in 31,500 mean?

F   10

G   100

H   1,000

J   10,000

3 What does the 6 in 65,724 mean?

A   60

B   600

C   6,000

D   60,000

4 What does the 8 in 32,872 mean?

F   80

G   800

H   8,000

J   80,000

5 Which number shows a 7 in the tens place?

A   93,076

B   79,304

C   43,708

D   35,047

6 Which number shows a 2 in the thousands place?

F   51,230

G   62,941

H   20,355

J   74,028

7 Which number shows a 5 in the ones place?

A   5,164

B   1,835

C   7,050

D   6,501

8 What does the 2 in 6,127 mean?

F   20

G   200

H   2,000

J   20,000

9 What does the 4 in 78,741 mean?

A   4

B   40

C   400

D   4,000

10 Which number shows a 1 in the hundreds place?

F   1,520

G   2,051

H   5,102

J   5,210

11 Which number shows a 3 in the tens place?

A   12,153

B   20,342

C   43,500

D   76,130

Check your answers on page 118.

Recognize Numbers

The owner of a car you want to buy says he's put only "nine thousand eight hundred two miles" on the car while he has owned it. You check the odometer. It reads 9,802. You know he is telling the truth because the digits on the odometer match his words.

Example Write the different forms for the number 2,436.

1,000s	100s	10s	1s
2	4	3	6

Step 1. Read the number across the place-value chart from left to right using digits and words.

2 thousands, 4 hundreds, 3 tens, 6 ones

Step 2. Write the number using digits only.

2,000 + 400 + 30 + 6

Step 3. Write the number using words only.

two thousand four hundred thirty-six

All of these forms are equal in value:
  2 thousands, 4 hundreds, 3 tens, 6 ones
  two thousand four hundred thirty-six
  2,000 + 400 + 30 + 6
  2,436

Example Look at the chart below to see the greatest decimal number that is less than 0 that can be created using the digits 0, 2, 5, and 7 once each.

ones 1	.	tenths 0.1	hundredths 0.01	thousandths 0.001	ten-thousandths 0.0001
0	.	7	5	2	0

Step 1. To create the decimal number with the **greatest value**, place the digit with the **greatest** value in the place that has the **greatest** value. Therefore, the **7** goes in the **tenths** place, which has the greatest value in a decimal number.

Step 2. Then place the next greatest digit, 5, in the place with the next greatest value, the **hundredths** place. Next place the 2 in the **thousandths** place.

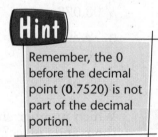

Hint

Remember, the 0 before the decimal point (**0.7520**) is not part of the decimal portion.

Step 3. Since **0** has the **least** value it should go as far to the **right** as possible. Place the **0** in the **ten-thousandths place**.

The decimal with the greatest value is 0.7520.

To create the decimal number with the **least** value, place the digit with the **least** value in the place with the **greatest** value. Therefore, start by placing the **0** in the **tenths** place. Place the **2** in the **hundredths** place, the **5** in the **thousandths** place and the **7** in the **ten-thousandths** place.

The decimal with the least value is 0.0257.

Applied Math

Read the question. Circle the answer.

1 Using the digits 0, 1, 5, and 9 only once, which of the following are the largest and smallest decimal numbers you can write?

A 0.9510 and 0.0159

B 0.9150 and 0.0519

C 0.9501 and 0.0195

D 0.9510 and 0.0195

1 A **0.9510 and 0.0159** 0.9510 is the greatest decimal because the **greatest digits** are in the places with the greatest value. 0.0159 is the least number because the digits with the **least value** are in the places with the greatest value.

Practice

Read the questions. Circle the answers.

1 Which of these is the same as the number in the place-value chart?

1,000s	100s	10s	1s
5	0	4	2

A 5,402

B 5,000 + 40 + 2

C 5 thousands 4 hundreds 2 tens

D five thousand four hundred two

2 Which of these is the same as the number in the place-value chart?

1,000s	100s	10s	1s
3	9	1	0

F three thousand nine hundred ten

G three thousand nine hundred ten zero

H 3,091

J 3,911

3 What are the greatest and least decimal numbers you can make using the digits 0, 1, 3, and 2 once?

A 0.3120 and 0.2013

B 0.3201 and 0.1032

C 0.3201 and 0.0123

D 0.3210 and 0.0123

4 Using the digits 0, 1, 4, and 7 only once, which of the following are the greatest and least decimal numbers you can write?

F 0.7140 and 0.0471

G 0.7410 and 0.0471

H 0.7401 and 0.0417

J 0.7410 and 0.0147

Check your answers on page 118.

Lesson 3 Money

When you write a check, you write numbers in different ways. You use digits ($35.15), words (thirty-five dollars and fifteen cents), or a combination of words and digits (thirty-five and $\frac{15}{100}$).

Example Look at the underlined numbers on the check below. Notice the different ways that numbers are written.

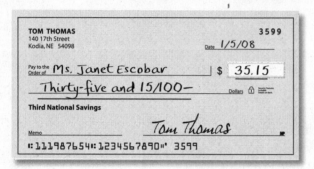

On checks, the amount is always written twice—once in digits with a decimal for the cents, and once in words with a fraction for the cents.

$35.15 means the same as *Thirty-five and $\frac{15}{100}$*.

Example The way a number is written depends on the best way to communicate a number.

David—Here's $50 change. Could you please go to the bank and exchange this for bills? I'd like:

> 4 tens
> 1 five
> 5 ones
>
> Thanks!
> Love, sherry

Sherry chose to write *5 ones* instead of *5 1s*, which could look like the number 51.

> **TABE Strategy**
>
> A decimal point in a dollar amount means "and __ out of 100." If you "read" the decimal this way, it is easy to rewrite the number as a fraction.

Test Example

Read the question. Circle the answer.

1 A customer bought a round trip ticket for $200.15. How should this number be written on a check to pay for the trip?

A Twenty and $\frac{15}{100}$ C Two hundred and $\frac{15}{100}$

B Twenty and $\frac{50}{100}$ D Two hundred and $\frac{50}{100}$

1 **C Two hundred and $\frac{15}{100}$.** The total cost for one person is $200.15. Option A equals $20.15. Option B equals $20.50. Option D would be written as $200.50.

Study the check below. Answer questions 1 and 2. Circle the answers.

LATONYA HAYNES
2705 Fifth Street
Pleasantville, NE 54009

Date *3-28-08*

5001

Pay to the
Order of *Ms Estelle Harris*

$ *16.50*

Dollars

Security Features
Included.
Details on Back.

First National Bank

Memo

LaTonya Hayes

MP

⑈314987104⑈1234567890⑈ 5001

1 LaTonya has to write the amount in the blank space on the check above. Which should she write on her check?

A Sixteen and $\frac{15}{100}$

B Sixty and $\frac{50}{100}$

C Sixty and $\frac{16}{100}$

D Sixteen and $\frac{50}{100}$

2 LaTonya has to write another check in the amount of $42.75. Which of these should be written on her check?

F Forty-two and $\frac{75}{100}$

G Forty and $\frac{75}{100}$

H Forty and $\frac{42}{100}$

J Forty-two and $\frac{42}{100}$

Read questions 3 and 4. Circle the answers.

3 Roberto received a refund check for $70.10. Which of these should be written on the check?

A Seventy and $\frac{70}{100}$

B Seventy and $\frac{00}{100}$

C Seventeen and $\frac{10}{100}$

D Seventy and $\frac{10}{100}$

4 Lisa wrote a check for her grocery purchase. She wrote "twenty-three and $\frac{65}{100}$ dollars" on the amount line. Which number should she write after the dollar sign?

F 20.65

G 23.65

H 32.65

J 65.23

Check your answers on page 118.

Lesson 4 · Fractional Parts

Every day you express numbers in fractional parts. Some examples are $\frac{1}{3}$ of a cup, a quarter of an hour, or a half-price sale. On the TABE you will solve problems with fractional parts.

Example **What fraction of the original price of a man's shirt is the sale price?**

Step 1. Write a fraction. $\frac{12}{24}$ ← part of the total / ← total

The fraction $\frac{12}{24}$ represents the sale price of the shirt.

Step 2. Reduce the fraction. To reduce the fraction, divide the top and the bottom numbers of the fraction by the same number.

$$\frac{12}{24} \div \frac{6}{6} = \frac{2}{4}$$

The reduced fraction is $\frac{2}{4}$.

Step 3. Reduce to lowest terms. The fraction has been reduced to its lowest terms when no number except 1 will divide evenly into both the top and bottom number. You can reduce $\frac{2}{4}$ to even lower terms. Try dividing each number by 2.

$$\frac{2}{4} \div \frac{2}{2} = \frac{1}{2}$$

The fraction reduced to lowest terms is $\frac{1}{2}$.

The sale price of the shirt is $\frac{1}{2}$ of the original price.

Example **Deb had $40. About how much of her total did Deb spend on one man's shirt?**

Step 1. The word *about* means you can estimate, or round. To *estimate* means to figure out an approximate value for a number, to make it easier to work with. For example, $12 rounds down to $10.

Step 2. Write a fraction. $\frac{10}{40}$

Step 3. Reduce the fraction to lowest terms.

$$\frac{10}{40} \div \frac{10}{10} = \frac{1}{4}$$

$12 is about $\frac{1}{4}$ of $40. Deb spent about $\frac{1}{4}$ of her money on a shirt.

Applied Math

Read the questions. Circle the answers.

1   Jane's yearly budget for clothes is $1,120. She buys a coat for $140. What fraction of her budget is the cost of the coat?

A $\frac{1}{10}$ C $\frac{1}{4}$

B $\frac{1}{8}$ D $\frac{1}{2}$

TABE Strategy

To find the correct answer on the TABE, make sure you have reduced the fraction to its lowest terms. You may need to divide more than once.

1   **B** $\frac{1}{8}$ The coat is $\frac{140}{1,120}$ of Jane's budget. That fraction can be reduced as follows:

$$\frac{140}{1,120} \div \frac{10}{10} = \frac{14}{112}$$

$$\frac{14}{112} \div \frac{7}{7} = \frac{2}{16}$$

$$\frac{2}{16} \div \frac{2}{2} = \frac{1}{8}$$

Practice

Study the list of ingredients for peanut butter cookies. Read the questions. Circle the answers.

Peanut Butter Cookies

You need:

6 tablespoons butter

$\frac{3}{4}$ cup peanut butter

1 egg

$\frac{3}{4}$ cup brown sugar

2 tablespoons vanilla extract

$1\frac{1}{2}$ cups flour

$\frac{3}{4}$ teaspoon baking soda

2   A bottle of vanilla extract holds 16 tablespoons. What fraction of a bottle of vanilla extract is needed?

F $\frac{2}{4}$ H $\frac{1}{8}$

G $\frac{1}{16}$ J $\frac{1}{4}$

3   You used $\frac{1}{6}$ of your eggs. How many eggs did you start with?

A 6

B 8

C 10

D 12

1   A stick of butter has 8 tablespoons. What fraction of a stick of butter is needed for the recipe?

A $\frac{1}{3}$ C $\frac{1}{2}$

B $\frac{3}{4}$ D $\frac{2}{3}$

Check your answers on page 118.

Operational Sense

You solve math problems by using operations such as adding, subtracting, dividing, and multiplying. When you read a problem, find the numbers and then decide what operation to use. Sometimes you also have to decide the order of the numbers.

Example **Curtis bought 4 boxes of tomatoes. Each box contains 8 tomatoes. How many tomatoes did he buy?**

Step 1. Find what numbers are used.

    4 boxes

    8 tomatoes

Step 2. Decide what operation to use.

    The question asks for the total number of tomatoes, so you will multiply the number of tomatoes in a box by the number of boxes.

    8×4

Step 3. Solve the operation

    $8 \times 4 = 32$ tomatoes

Test Example

Read the question. Circle the answer.

1 Lindsay used 3 candles from a pack of 12. Which expression shows how many candles are left?

    A $12 - 3$

    B $12 \div 3$

    C $3 - 12$

    D $3 + 12$

Hint

Think about whether the number should get larger or smaller. Also think about whether the problem deals with groups.

1 **A** **$12 - 3$** After using 3 candles, Lindsay has fewer candles than the original number. The number of remaining candles is found by subtracting the used candles from the starting number.

Read the questions. Circle the answers.

1 Lisa had 3 dogs. She just got 6 puppies. Which expression shows how many dogs Lisa has now?

A 3 + 6

B 3 × 6

C 6 − 3

D 6 ÷ 3

2 There were 12 cans of soup on a store shelf. Frank unpacked 24 more cans and placed them on the shelf. Which expression shows the total number of cans of soup?

F 24 ÷ 12

G 24 + 12

H 24 + 24

J 24 − 12

3 A group of 100 students are traveling by bus to a museum. If there are 4 buses, which expression shows how many students should ride on each bus?

A 100 − 4

B 100 ÷ 4

C 4 + 100

D 4 × 100

4 Mike had checked out 10 library books. He returned 6 of the books. Which expression shows the number of books he still has checked out?

F 10 + 6

G 10 × 6

H 10 − 6

J 10 ÷ 6

5 A box of pencils holds 12 pencils. There are 36 boxes in a case. Which expression shows the number of pencils in a case?

A 36 × 12

B 36 ÷ 12

C 36 − 12

D 36 + 12

6 There are 40 children at the day-care center where Sherena works. Of these, 13 come only to the after-school program. The rest stay all day. Which expression shows the number of students who stay all day?

F 13 + 40

G 13 × 40

H 40 − 13

J 40 ÷ 13

7 On a particular morning, 5 cars are at a tire store. Each car needs 4 tires replaced. Which expression shows how many tires need to be replaced in all?

A 5 − 4

B 5 ÷ 4

C 4 + 5

D 4 × 5

8 There are 16 pieces of peach pie to be shared by 8 people. Which expression shows the number of pieces each person should get?

F 16 + 8

G 16 − 8

H 16 ÷ 8

J 16 × 8

Check your answers on page 118.

Operational Properties

You have a dozen eggs. Your neighbor borrows a few and you find that you have 7 eggs left. You ask your neighbor to return the exact number to add up to a dozen. How many did he take? How many does he need to return? These are word sentences that can be solved by converting them into number sentences.

Example How many eggs did your neighbor borrow? How many eggs does your neighbor need to return?

Step 1. Find your key facts. You had 12 eggs to start. Now you have 7 eggs left.

Step 2. Write a number sentence using the information you have.

$12 - \square = 7$ The empty box stands for the number of eggs your neighbor borrowed.

$7 + \square = 12$ The box stands for the number of eggs your neighbor needs to return.

Step 3. Find the missing number in the first sentence by subtracting 7 from 12 to find the difference. The completed sentence is: $12 - 5 = 7$.

Step 4. If you add 5 to 7 to get to 12, then 5 makes the second sentence true. Does $7 + 5 = 12$? Yes, it does.

The number 5 makes both number sentences true. $12 - 5 = 7$ and $7 + 5 = 12$. **Your neighbor borrowed 5 eggs and needs to return 5 eggs.**

Test Example

Read the question. Circle the answer.

1   If the same number is used in both boxes, which of these statements would be true?

    A If $3 + 6 = \square$, then $\square + 3 = 6$

    B If $\square + 4 = 9$, then $\square - 4 = 9$

    C If $15 - \square = 6$, then $\square - 6 = 15$

    D If $12 - \square = 6$, then $6 + \square = 12$

1   D If **$12 - \square = 6$, then $6 + \square = 12$.** 6 subtracted from 12 equals 6, which is the correct answer for the first part of the statement. If 6 is added to the second statement, it becomes $6 + 6 = 12$, which is also true. Options A, B, and C are incorrect because the numbers in each box are not the same. For example, in B, $\underline{5} + 4 = 9$ is true, but $\underline{5} - 4 = 9$ is not a true statement.

Read the questions. Circle the answers.

1 What number goes in the boxes to make both number sentences true?

$17 - \square = 9$
$9 + \square = 17$

A 9
B 8
C 7
D 16

2 What number goes in the boxes to make both number sentences true?

$13 - \square = 8$
$8 + \square = 13$

F 5
G 8
H 21
J 6

3 If the same number is used in both boxes, which of these statements would be true?

A If $12 - \square = 5$, then $5 + \square = 12$.
B If $\square + 4 = 7$, then $\square - 4 = 7$.
C If $4 + 5 = \square$, then $\square + 4 = 5$.
D If $14 - \square = 7$, then $\square - 7 = 14$.

4 What number goes in the boxes to make both number sentences true?

$9 + \square = 18$
$18 - \square = 9$

F 8
G 9
H 10
J 27

5 If the same number is used in both boxes, which of these statements would be true?

A If $14 - \square = 6$, then $6 + 14 = \square$.
B If $9 + \square = 11$, then $11 + \square = 9$.
C If $7 - 3 = \square$, then $7 + \square = 3$.
D If $6 + \square = 8$, then $8 - \square = 6$.

6 What number goes in the boxes to make both number sentences true?

$9 + \square = 14$
$14 - \square = 9$

F 5
G 6
H 15
J 19

7 What number goes in the boxes to make both number sentences true?

$15 - \square = 9$
$9 + \square = 15$

A 9
B 6
C 8
D 24

TABE Strategy

Try each option in the first equation. Then try the number that works in the second equation.

Check your answers on pages 118–119.

Lesson 7 Equivalent Form

Look at the price of the sunflower seeds. The price also could be written as "98 cents" or "98¢." All three are equivalent forms. This price can be written as: $0.98, 98 cents, and 98¢.

Sunflower seeds
$0.98 per pound

You will find problems on the TABE that include different ways to express a number.

Example Dollar amounts can be written in different forms.
Peppers are $0.79 per pound. What is another way to show this amount?

Step 1. In dollar amounts, look for the decimal point ($0.79).

Step 2. The numbers to the left of the decimal tell you how many dollars. The numbers to the right tell you how many cents.

Step 3. There are 0 dollars and 79 cents in the price as shown.

Other ways to write $0.79 are "79 cents" and "79¢."

Example Numbers can also be written in equivalent form using addition and subtraction.
Which is not an equivalent form of the number 8?
4 + 4   9 − 1   2 + 5

Step 1. Add or subtract each number sentence.

4 + 4 = 8
9 − 1 = 8
2 + 5 = 7

Step 2. Compare answers. The third form does not equal 8.

Since 2 + 5 = 7, the sum of 2 + 5 is not an equivalent form of 8.

Test Example

Read the question. Circle the answers.

1   How much do apples cost per pound?

A   8 cents

B   9 cents

C   89 cents

D   90 cents

APPLES
$0.89 per pound

1   **C 89 cents** is an equivalent form for $0.89. Option A is $0.08. Option B is $0.09, and option D is $0.90.

Applied Math

Study the phone bill. Answer numbers 1 and 2.

Domestic Long Distance

▶ Total Domestic Long Distance Charges........$ 1.25
Service Charge... 1.02
Carrier Property Tax... .12
Federal Tax... .36
Toll calls have changed from $0.20 to $0.25 per minute.

1 What is the new cost of toll calls?

A 2 cents

B 5 cents

C 25 cents

D 20 cents

2 What is the federal tax?

F 36 cents

G 6 cents

H 3 cents

J 12 cents

Read the questions. Circle the answers.

3 Which number sentence does not have an answer of 8 when you solve it?

A 7 + 2 = ☐

B 9 − 1 = ☐

C 10 − 2 = ☐

D 5 + 3 = ☐

4 Which number sentence does not have an answer of 6 when you solve it?

F 5 + 1 = ☐

G 3 + 3 = ☐

H 9 − 3 = ☐

J 7 − 3 = ☐

5 Which number sentence has an answer of 9?

A 9 + 2 = ☐

B 11 − 2 = ☐

C 11 − 9 = ☐

D 7 − 2 = ☐

6 Which of the following is not an equivalent form of the number 7?

F 4 + 3

G 9 − 3

H 12 − 5

J 7 + 0

7 Which of the following is an equivalent form of $0.09?

A nine cents

B ninety cents

C nine dollars

D ninety dollars

Check your answers on page 119.

Lesson 8 — Multiples and Divisibility

Maria has 32 crayons to use when she baby-sits. Today she is baby-sitting 6 children. Maria wants to give each child the same number of crayons. To figure out how many each gets, she can divide the number of crayons by 6 ($32 \div 6 = 5$, with 2 left over). The amount left is called a **remainder**. Each child gets 5 crayons. There are 2 left over crayons.

A larger number that can be divided by a smaller number with no remainder is a multiple of the smaller number.

Example Solve using division.

Stan has 28 chicken nuggets and 5 friends. How can he divide the nuggets equally among his friends?

Step 1. Decide which number you will divide by. Draw 5 squares to stand for the 5 friends.

Step 2. Decide which number is to be divided. There are 28 nuggets to be divided up equally among the friends. Draw 1 circle to stand for each chicken nugget.

$28 \div 5 = 5$ R 3. **Each friend will get an equal share of 5, with a remainder of 3 chicken nuggets.**

Test Example

Read the question. Circle the answer.

1 Jamal has 13 light bulbs. Each of the light fixtures in his house needs 2 bulbs. How many light fixtures can be completely filled with light bulbs?

 A 1

 B 2

 C 3

 D 6

> **TABE Strategy**
>
> To solve a division problem, first find the number you will divide by. Then find the number to be divided into.

1 D 6 $13 \div 2 = 6$, with a remainder of 1. Jamal can replace 6 fixtures with 2 bulbs each. There will be 1 bulb left over.

Applied Math

Read the questions. Circle the answers.

1 Roz planted 37 seeds in trays. Each tray has space for 6 seeds. How many completely full trays does Roz have?

A 3

B 4

C 5

D 6

2 George replaced 40 windowpanes. Each window required 8 panes. How many windows was George able to replace completely?

F 5

G 6

H 7

J 8

3 Michael has 13 CDs he would like to play. His CD player holds 5 CDs. How many times can he completely fill his CD player with CDs?

A 4

B 3

C 2

D 1

4 Lisa is arranging rides to a party for 26 friends. Each car will hold 5 people. How many cars will be completely full?

F 4

G 5

H 6

J 7

5 Carla put 33 oranges into paper bags. Each bag holds 5 oranges. How many completely full bags did Carla have?

A 4

B 5

C 6

D 7

6 Which number is a multiple of 4?

F 6

G 12

H 14

J 18

7 Which of these is a multiple of 5?

A 11

B 18

C 20

D 24

8 Which of these numbers is a multiple of 7?

F 17

G 21

H 27

J 30

9 Which number has a remainder when divided by 3?

A 9

B 15

C 18

D 23

Check your answers on page 119.

Lesson 9   Factors

You ordered two pizzas to be evenly divided among your family of 6. The small pizza is cut into 12 slices. The large pizza is cut into 24 slices. There is enough for each family member to get 2 slices of the small pizza (12 ÷ 6 = 2). Everyone can also have 4 slices of the large pizza (24 ÷ 6 = 4). A **common factor** for 12 and 24 is 6.

A number is a **factor** of another number if it divides into that number **evenly**. If two numbers are both divisible by the same number, this number is a common factor. On the TABE you will be asked to find a common factor for two numbers.

Example   **Find the common factors of 8 and 12.**

Step 1. Think of numbers that can divide into 8 without a remainder.

8 ÷ 1 = 8
8 ÷ 2 = 4
8 ÷ 4 = 2
8 ÷ 8 = 1

Therefore, 1, 2, 4, and 8 are the factors of 8.

Step 2. Think of the numbers that can divide into 12 without a remainder.

12 ÷ 1 = 12
12 ÷ 2 = 6
12 ÷ 3 = 4
12 ÷ 4 = 3
12 ÷ 6 = 2
12 ÷ 12 = 1

Therefore, 1, 2, 3, 4, 6, and 12 are the factors of 12.

Step 3. Identify the factors that are common to both 8 and 12.

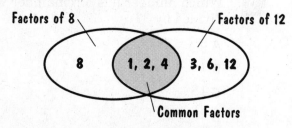

The common factors for 8 and 12 are 1, 2, and 4.

Test Example

Read the question. Circle the answer.

1   Which of these numbers is a common factor of 24 and 32?

    A   3   C   5

    B   4   D   6

TABE Strategy

Divide each number by each answer choice until you find a common factor. 24 ÷ 3 = ?, 32 ÷ 3 = ?, etc.

1   **B**   **4** Only 4 can be multiplied together with another number to get 24 and 32. Options A, C, and D are incorrect because 3, 5, and 6 cannot be multiplied with another number to get both 24 and 32.

Read the questions. Circle the answers.

1 Which set of numbers shows the factors of 9?

A 1, 3, 9

B 9, 18, 27

C 9, 19, 29

D 1, 10, 19

2 Which set of numbers show the factors of 16?

F 2, 8, 16

G 4, 10, 16

H 16, 32, 48, 64

J 1, 2, 4, 8, 16

3 Which of these numbers is a common factor of 22 and 88?

A 8

B 9

C 10

D 11

4 Which of these numbers is a common factor of 24 and 40?

F 6

G 7

H 8

J 9

5 Which of these numbers is a common factor of 20 and 36?

A 3

B 4

C 5

D 6

6 Which of these numbers is a common factor of 49 and 56?

F 6

G 7

H 8

J 4

7 Carlos put 27 eggs in cartons. Each carton holds 6 eggs. How many cartons will be completely full of eggs?

A 7

B 6

C 5

D 4

8 Which number is a common factor of 18 and 30?

F 3

G 4

H 8

J 9

9 What number goes in the boxes to make both number sequences true?

$15 - \square = 7$
$7 + \square = 15$

A 6

B 7

C 8

D 9

10 Which number is a common factor of 48 and 60?

F 8

G 9

H 12

J 16

Check your answers on page 119.

Lesson 10 — Number Line

You can use a number line to show the relationships between whole numbers. A number line is a line that has points at regular intervals, and each point has an assigned value. On the TABE you will solve problems using a number line.

Example What number goes in the box on the number line?

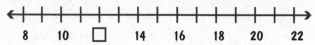

Step 1. First decide on the value of each point along the number line. Each point is 1 and the box is 2 points beyond 10. 10 is 2 more than 8. Add 2 + 10 = 12.

Step 2. To make sure that 2 is the correct interval, add 2 to 12 to see if it will equal the next number. 12 + 2 = 14. Each point on the number line is 2 more than the one to the left of it.

12 should go in the box on the number line.

Test Example

Read the question. Circle the answer.

1   What number goes in the box on the number line?

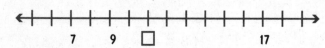

A   13

B   11

C   10

D   16

Hint

Check your answer by comparing it to a third point on the number line.

1   B Each point on the number line is 1 more than the one to the left of it. The box is 2 points beyond 9. 9 + 2 = 11.

Applied Math

Read the question. Circle the answer.

1 What number goes in the box on the number line?

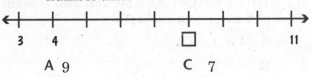

A 9		**C** 7	
B 8		**D** 10	

2 What number goes in the box on the number line?

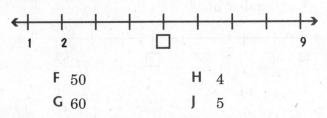

F 50		**H** 4	
G 60		**J** 5	

3 What number goes in the box on the number line?

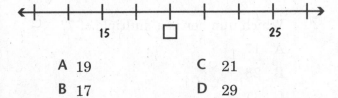

A 19		**C** 21	
B 17		**D** 29	

4 What number goes in the box on the number line?

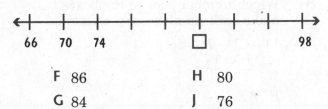

F 86		**H** 80	
G 84		**J** 76	

5 What number goes in the box on the number line?

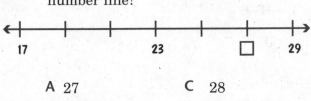

A 27		**C** 28	
B 26		**D** 25	

6 What number goes in the box on the number line?

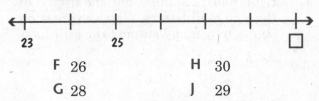

F 26		**H** 30	
G 28		**J** 29	

7 Amos recorded daily rainfall totals for the past five days on this chart.

Weekly Rainfall

Day	Total Snowfall for week
Monday	2 inches
Tuesday	3 inches
Wednesday	6 inches
Thursday	8 inches
Friday	10 inches

He wanted to use a number line to plot the amount and the day. Which day would be at 6?

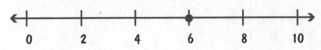

A Monday		**C** Thursday	
B Wednesday		**D** Tuesday	

8 What number goes in the box on the number line?

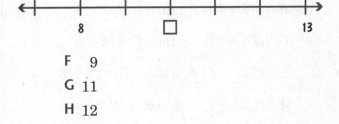

F 9

G 11

H 12

J 10

Check your answers on page 119.

Read the question. Circle the answer.

1   Lynn had 12 stamps, but she used 3 of them to mail letters. Which expression shows how many stamps she still has?

A 3×12

B $12 \div 3$

C $12 - 3$

D $3 + 12$

2   Luis has 19 soft drink cans. His coolers each have space for 6 cans. How many coolers can he fill completely?

F   3

G   4

H   5

J   6

3   Which of these numbers is a common factor of 18 and 24?

A   3

B   4

C   5

D   7

4   If the same number is used in both boxes, which of these statements would be true?

F   If $2 + 5 = \Box$, then $\Box + 2 = 5$

G   If $4 + \Box = 8$, then $\Box + 4 = 8$

H   If $12 - \Box = 6$, then $\Box - 12 = 6$

J   If $18 - \Box = 8$, then $\Box - 18 = 8$

5   Which number does *not* have an answer of 5 when you solve it?

A $4 + 1 = \Box$

B $2 + 3 = \Box$

C $9 - 4 = \Box$

D $8 - 4 = \Box$

6   Which number goes in the box on the number line?

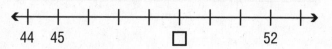

44   45 $\Box$ 52

F   49

G   50

H   48

J   51

7   Which number is a multiple of 7?

A   17

B   28

C   37

D   45

8   Which number goes in the boxes to make both number sentences true?

$11 - \Box = 7$

$7 + \Box = 11$

F   4

G   5

H   6

J   7

This price list shows the costs of vegetables at the farmer's market. Study the price list. Then answer numbers 9 and 10.

Vegetable Prices

Tomatoes $0.72 per pound
Carrots $0.59 per pound
Lettuce $0.98 per pound

9 The cost of carrots per pound is

A 59 dollars

B 72 dollars

C 59 cents

D 98 cents

10 The cost of tomatoes per pound is

F 2 cents

G 7 cents

H 59 cents

J 72 cents

Read the questions. Circle the answers.

11 What number goes in the boxes to make both number sentences true?

$16 - \square = 8$

$8 + \square = 16$

A 5

B 6

C 7

D 8

12 Which number goes in the box on the number line?

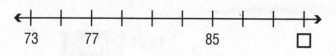

F 89

G 91

H 93

J 87

13 Marty needs to pack 32 glasses. Each box holds 6 glasses. How many boxes will be completely full?

A 4

B 5

C 6

D 7

14 Lee has finished reading 4 out of 10 lessons from his assignment. Which fractional part of the lessons has he completed?

F $\frac{1}{10}$ H $\frac{2}{3}$

G $\frac{1}{5}$ J $\frac{2}{5}$

15 Which number sentence does <u>not</u> have an answer of nine?

A $8 + 1 = \square$

B $11 - 2 = \square$

C $12 - 3 = \square$

D $3 + 4 = \square$

Check your answers on page 119.

Lesson 11 Charts

Whenever you read a newspaper or a magazine, you are likely to see a table, chart, or diagram. A stock market column or a baseball standing are examples of tables. Information presented this way gives the reader a quick understanding of a group of numbers.

On the TABE, you'll be asked to interpret many kinds of information presented in tables, charts, and diagrams.

Example How much has Jay paid for repairs on his car during the last four months?

	A	B Jan	C Feb	D March	E April
1		Jan	Feb	March	April
2	Gas	$67.36	$72.60	$71.50	$85.30
3	Insurance	$122.00	$122.00	$122.00	$122.00
4	Repairs	$0.00	$382.70	$0.00	$106.00
5	Tows	$0.00	$75.00	$0.00	$75.00

Car Expenses — Sheet1 / Sheet2 / Sheet3 — Ready

Step 1. Find the *Repairs* heading in the column at the left.

Step 2. Look across the *Repairs* row to find the repair cost for each month.

Step 3. Add the costs for each month.

$0.00 + $382.70 + $0.00 + $106.00 = $488.70

Jay's total repair expense for the last four months was $488.70.

Test Example

Read the question. Circle the answer.

1 How much did Jay spend on his car in February?

A $123.50

B $189.36

C $488.00

D $652.30

TABE Strategy

Read row headings across from left to right and column headings from top to bottom to find information.

1 D **$652.30** In the column for February, the amount for gas is $72.60, the cost of insurance is $122.00, repairs are $382.70, and a tow is $75.00. Add the amounts. The total is $652.30.

Use Jay's table on page 36 to answer number 1.

1 What did Jay spend on insurance January through April?

A $122   C $244

B $296   D $488

Study this diagram of the places Caroline visits on a weekly basis. The diagram shows the miles between the stops in her weekly routine. Answer numbers 2 and 3.

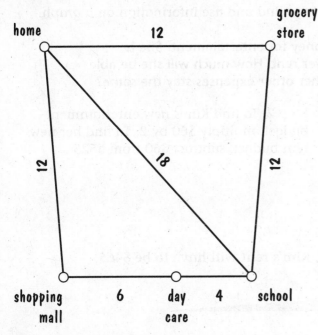

2 What is the distance from home to school, stopping by the grocery store on the way?

F 12 miles   H 22 miles

G 18 miles   J 24 miles

3 From home, Caroline stops by the shopping mall and the day care center on her way to school, but she takes the shortest way back. How many miles does she travel all together?

A 22 miles   C 40 miles

B 18 miles   D 42 miles

Study this information on placing classified advertisements. Answer numbers 4 and 5.

THE DAILY SUN   Classified Ads

To place a classified ad:

☎ **Call:** 312 555-5555   Monday–Friday 8 a.m. to 5 p.m.

🖱 **Online:** Buy-Sell.com

3 lines/7 days $27.00 $8.45 for each additional line

3 lines/14 days $50.00 $15.85 for each additional line

Your ad will appear in our daily paper and on Buy-Sell.com Call for details.

4 How much money is saved by running an ad for 14 days instead of running the same ad for two 7-day periods?

F $2.75   H $23.00

G $4.00   J $50.00

5 What does it cost to run two 4-line ads for 14 days?

A $35.45   C $100.00

B $65.85   D $131.70

Check your answers on pages 119–120.

Lesson 12 Graphs

The following circle graph shows how Kim spends her monthly income.

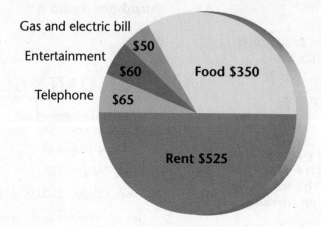

Gas and electric bill $50

Entertainment $60

Telephone $65

Food $350

Rent $525

Some questions on the TABE will test your ability to find and use information on a graph.

Example **Kim wants to budget twice as much money for entertainment. She is thinking about finding a place with lower rent. How much will she be able to spend on entertainment and rent if her other expenses stay the same?**

Step 1. Read the graph. What does Kim currently pay for rent? **$525**. How much does she spend on entertainment? **$60**.

Step 2. To find Kim's new entertainment budget, multiply $60 by 2. To find her new rent budget, subtract $60 from $525.

Step 3. Work the problems.

Entertainment: $60 × 2 = $120
Rent: $525 − $60 = $465

To increase her entertainment amount to $120, Kim's rent will have to be $465.

Test Example

Read the question. Circle the answer.

1 Instead of moving to a new place, Kim thinks about cutting her food budget in order to double her entertainment amount. If she does this, how much money would she have for food each month?

   A $460

   B $290

   C $400

   D $340

 Hint

If money is added to one part of a budget, it has to be subtracted from another.

1   **B $290** If Kim doubles her entertainment amount, she needs $60. If she subtracts the $60 from her food amount of $350, the new budget would be $290.

Applied Math

Study the graph. Answers numbers 1 through 5.

Kim's New Monthly Budget

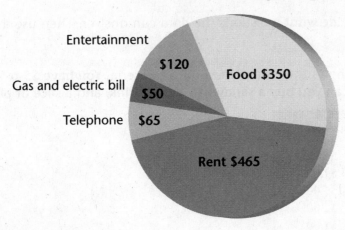

Entertainment $120

Gas and electric bill $50

Telephone $65

Food $350

Rent $465

1 Kim decides to move because in the summer, her gas and electric bill doubles. She will have to use the extra money she needs from her food allowance to cover this bill. How much will she have for food each month during the summer?

A $400

B $250

C $290

D $300

2 According to the graph, what does Kim pay for rent in a year?

F $1,440

G $5,580

H $3,120

J $3,200

3 According to the graph, how many months will it take for Kim to spend $480 on entertainment?

A 2

B 3

C 4

D 5

4 About what fraction of her total budget does Kim spend for rent each month?

F $\frac{1}{6}$

G $\frac{1}{4}$

H $\frac{1}{3}$

J $\frac{1}{2}$

5 Kim decides to put $\frac{1}{3}$ of her entertainment amount into a savings account each month. How much will she put in savings each month?

A $30

B $40

C $50

D $60

Check your answers on page 120.

Lesson 13 Conclusions from Data

Charts and graphs are ways to show information. The information on a chart or graph is called data. You can use this data to make conclusions. A conclusion may explain how things affect one another. Sometimes a conclusion can lead to a decision.

To come to a conclusion, decide what questions the data can answer. Then use the data to determine the right answer.

Example The chart below shows the cost of items at a cafeteria. You have $5 to spend for lunch. Can you buy a sandwich, a cold drink, and a slice of pie?

Item	Cost
Sandwich	$2.00
Cold drink	$1.00
Fruit	$1.00
Vegetable	$1.00
Pie	$2.00
Coffee	$1.00

Step 1. Decide what information you need to answer your question.

You need to know the cost of each item that you want to buy.

Step 2. Find the information on the chart.

The costs of the items you want are:

$2 for a sandwich
$1 for a drink
$2 for a slice of pie

Step 3. Make a conclusion that answers your question.

The total cost of the items is:
$2 + $1 + $2 = $5
This amount is equal to $5.

You conclude that you have enough money.

Test Example

Read the question. Circle the answer.

1   What is the cost of a slice of pie, coffee, and a piece of fruit?

   A $2   C $5

   B $4   D $6

Hint

Think about how the data can be used to answer a question.

1   **B $4** You can find the cost by looking at each cost and adding. Pie costs $2, fruit costs $1, and coffee costs $1. You conclude the total cost is $4.

Read the questions. Circle the answers.

A manager needs to schedule drivers to make deliveries. Study this information about the number of drivers needed each day. Answer questions 1 and 2.

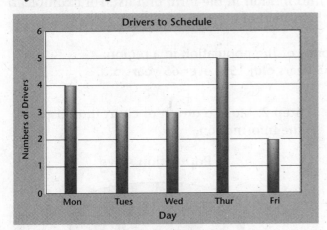

1 On which day will the fewest drivers be needed?

A Tuesday

B Wednesday

C Thursday

D Friday

2 What is the least number of drivers needed to make sure that there are enough drivers for every shift?

F 2

G 5

H 6

J 17

This chart shows some monthly expenses. Study the chart and answer questions 3 and 4.

Monthly budget

Expense	Amount
Rent	$450
Car Payment	$200
Gas	$50
Food	$200
Utilities	$100
Phone	$50

3 How much money should be budgeted for the car and gasoline expenses?

A $50

B $200

C $250

D $300

4 How much money is needed each month for the total expenses on the chart?

F $450

G $1,050

A $700

J $2,000

Check your answers on page 120.

Lesson 14 Appropriate Data Display

There are many different types of graphs and charts. When organizing information, choose an appropriate type of data display. If you want to show how a whole amount is broken into parts, such as percents, use a circle graph. To compare quantities, use a bar graph. A line graph is most useful to show a change over time.

Sometimes a chart is the best way to present information in the form of a list. For example, a list of prices is often displayed on a chart or table instead of a graph.

Example Make a graph that shows the age groups of the population in a region: 35% under 21 years old; 50% 21 to 65 years old; 15% over 65 years old.

Step 1. Decide what type of display to use.

This data could be shown on a chart or graph. Since you are showing the parts of a whole population, a circle graph would be useful.

Step 2. Make a graph or chart that displays the information.

Population Ages

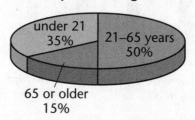

under 21 35% | 21–65 years 50%

65 or older 15%

Test Example

Read the question. Circle the answer.

1 Which type of display best shows changes in the temperature during the day?

    A circle graph

    B bar graph

    C line graph

    D diagram

Hint

When you make a graph or chart, always include a title.

1 **C line graph** To show changes over time, a line graph is the appropriate display.

Read the questions. Circle the answers.

1 Which type of display would be most appropriate to show the change in the number of customers at a store over a month?

   A line graph

   B circle graph

   C chart

   D bar graph

2 Which type of display would you use to compare how many birds of each kind come to a bird feeder?

   F line graph

   G bar graph

   H circle graph

   J chart

3 Which of the following would be the best display for a price list at a car repair shop?

   A line graph

   B circle graph

   C chart

   D bar graph

Jason asked 100 people how they get to work each day. He made the graph below to display his data. Study the graph and answer questions 4 and 5.

Tranportation to Work

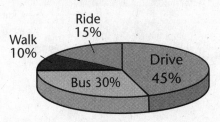

4 Which form of transportation did the greatest number of people use to get to work?

   F ride

   G walk

   H bus

   J drive

5 Why might Jason use a bar graph instead of a circle graph for this data?

   A to show how the different ways to get to work changes over time

   B to display a comparison of number of people who use each method of transportation

   C to compare the cost of different ways to get to work

   D to show how many people work each day

Check your answers on page 120.

This circle graph shows what Jim ate in one day and the calories in each of the foods. Read the graph. Answer numbers 1 and 2.

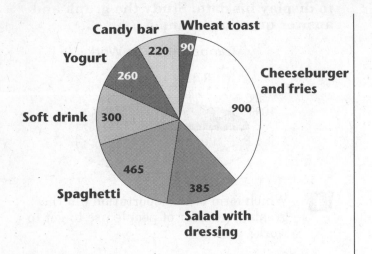

2 Suppose Jim had wanted a dessert with 520 calories, but he didn't want to add any more calories to his diet. What two items should he not eat?

F candy bar and soft drink

G salad and dressing

H spaghetti and toast

J toast and yogurt

1 According to the graph, how many slices of wheat toast can Jim eat and only consume 270 calories?

A 2   C 4

B 3   D 5

This graph shows average scores for five basketball players. Read the graph. Answer numbers 3 and 4.

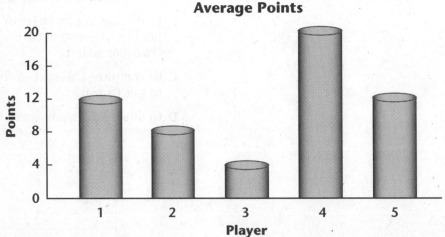

3 Which two players had the same average score?

A Players 1 and 2

B Players 2 and 3

C Players 3 and 4

D Players 1 and 5

4 The difference between average scores is greatest between which two players?

F Players 1 and 2

G Players 2 and 3

H Players 3 and 4

J Players 1 and 5

This is the table that Jay created to track his car expenses. Read the table. Answer numbers 5 and 6.

	A	B	C	D	E
1		Jan	Feb	March	April
2	Gas	$67.36	$72.60	$71.50	$85.30
3	Insurance	$122.00	$122.00	$122.00	$122.00
4	Repairs	$0.00	$382.70	$0.00	$106.00
5	Tows	$0.00	$75.00	$0.00	$75.00
6					
7					

Car Expenses — Sheet1 / Sheet2 / Sheet3 — Ready

5 Jay's monthly payment for a new car would be about $\frac{1}{2}$ of his repair expenses from January to April. Which of these could be the amount of Jay's monthly payment for a new car?

A $250.00

B $200.00

C $300.00

D $350.00

6 Recording monthly expenses for his car can help Jay decide

F the price of a new car

G if the garage is charging a fair price for towing

H his gas mileage

J if he is spending too much money to maintain his old car

Shamika is driving to a family reunion. This map shows the area between Harrisburg, where Shamika lives, and Bloomington, the reunion site. Study the map. Answer numbers 7 and 8.

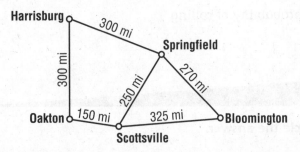

7 Shamika agrees to pick up relatives in Oakton and Scottsville. What is the distance from Harrisburg to Bloomington when driving through Oakton and Scottsville?

A 450 miles

B 550 miles

C 725 miles

D 775 miles

8 From Bloomington, Shamika and her relatives want to take a trip to Springfield. If she drives from Bloomington to Springfield, drops off her relatives in Oakton and Scottsville and returns to Harrisburg, how many miles will she travel going home?

F 270

G 570

H 850

J 970

Check your answers on page 120.

Lesson 15 **Probability**

A weather report states that the probability of rain is 20%. *Probability* is a measure of the chance of something happening. If an event is impossible, its probability is equal to zero. If the event is certain to happen, its probability is equal to 1. If something may or may not happen, the probability is stated as a fraction or a percent between 0 and 1.

To find a probability, you divide the ways a particular result, or *outcome*, can happen by the number of possible outcomes.

Example **You roll one die. What is the probability that you will roll an even number?**

Step 1. Find out how many ways the particular result can happen.

There are 3 even numbers, so there are 3 ways to roll an even number.

Step 2. Find out how many possible outcomes exist.

There are 6 numbers on a die, so there are 6 possible outcomes.

Step 3. Find the probability by dividing the ways the result can happen by the possible outcomes.

The probability of an even number is 3 divided by 6.

$\frac{3}{6} = \frac{1}{2}$. Therefore, the probability of rolling an even number is $\frac{1}{2}$.

Test Example

Read the question. Circle the answer.

1   A bag contains 8 marbles. Two of the marbles are green. If you pull 1 marble out of the bag, what is the probability that it is a green marble?

   A $\frac{1}{8}$ C $\frac{1}{2}$

   B $\frac{1}{4}$ D 1

Hint

Remember to change fractions to their simplest form.

1   B $\frac{1}{4}$ There are 2 green marbles and 8 marbles total, so the probability is $\frac{2}{8} = \frac{1}{4}$.

Read the questions. Circle the answers.

1 Someone randomly picks a day of the week. What is the probability that the day chosen will be a Wednesday?

A 0

B $\frac{1}{7}$

C $\frac{6}{7}$

D 1

2 You draw a letter tile in a word game. If there are 20 tiles and 4 of them have the letter E, what is the probability that you will draw an E?

F $\frac{1}{2}$

G $\frac{1}{5}$

H $\frac{1}{10}$

J $\frac{1}{20}$

3 If you flip a coin once, what is the probability it will land heads up?

A 0%

B 20%

C 50%

D 100%

4 You have 4 bills in your wallet: $1, $5, $10, and $20. If you pull one out at random, what is the probability that the bill is worth more than $8?

F $\frac{1}{2}$

G $\frac{1}{4}$

H 1

J 0

5 A bag holds 5 red marbles, 5 blue marbles, and 5 yellow marbles. What is the probability of drawing a red marble from the bag?

A $\frac{1}{15}$

B $\frac{1}{3}$

C $\frac{1}{2}$

D 1

6 In a certain rain forest, rain falls one-half the time. What is the probability of precipitation?

F 20%

G 40%

H 50%

J 90%

7 Out of 100 students at a school, 17 have red hair. What is the probability that the next student walking past the office will have red hair?

A 1%

B 17%

C 50%

D 83%

8 A game spinner is divided into 8 equal parts, numbered 1 through 8. What is the probability of spinning a 5?

F $\frac{1}{5}$

G $\frac{1}{4}$

H $\frac{1}{8}$

J $\frac{1}{3}$

Check your answers on page 120.

Lesson 16 Statistics

Sometimes you want to describe a group of numbers. One way to do that is to use the mean (often called the "average"). The mean is one number that describes all the numbers.

For example, the mean of height of adult men in the United States is 5 feet, 9 inches. Most men are either taller or shorter than that height. However, the mean height gives a very general description of the population.

To find a mean, add all the numbers together. Then divide the sum by how many numbers were added.

Example In her last four bowling games, Claire scores 180, 140, 145, and 175. What is the mean of her bowling scores?

Step 1. Find the sum of the scores. Regroup if you need to do so.

```
  180
  140
  145
 +175
  640
```

Step 2. Divide the sum by the number of scores

```
      160
   4)640
```

Her mean score is 160. This number represents how well she bowled in the four games. She did not score 160 in any one game.

Test Example

Read the question. Circle the answer.

1 Find the mean of this set of numbers: 4, 8, 6, 9, 8.

   A 4

   B 7

   C 8

   D 35

> **Hint**
>
> The mean is never greater than the largest value or less than the smallest value.

1 **B 7** The sum of the numbers is 35. There are 5 numbers. When you divide 35 by 5, you obtain a mean of 7.

Read the questions. Circle the answers.

1 Find the mean of this data set: 6, 8, 10.

A 5

B 6

C 8

D 9

2 The number of runs scored by a baseball team in its first six games were 4, 2, 0, 4, 1, and 1. What was the mean number of runs scored?

F 1

G 2

H 4

J 12

3 Sam's telephone bill shows that he made 5 calls on Sunday, 3 on Monday, 12 on Tuesday, and 4 calls on Wednesday. What was his mean number of calls per day?

A 4

B 6

C 10

D 24

4 You have a $5 bill and three $1 bills. What is the mean value of the 4 bills?

F $1

G $2

H $4

J $10

5 In his last four bowling games, Andrew scores 170, 150, 130, and 190. What is the mean of his bowling scores?

A 150

B 170

C 160

D 190

6 Gloria is going to put 87 apples into crates. Each crate holds 12 apples. How many crates will be completely full of apples?

F 6

G 7

H 8

J 9

The table below shows the number of airplanes manufactured at a plant for the first 4 months of the year. Study the table and answer questions 7 and 8.

Airplanes Manufactured in Plant	
Month	Number of Planes
February	12
March	15
April	9
May	12

7 What was the mean number of planes built each month?

A 12

B 15

C 4

D 8

8 If the mean does not change, how many planes can the plant manufacture in one year?

F 12

G 48

H 100

J 144

Check your answers on page 120.

Read the questions. Circle the answers.

1 Find the mean of this data set: 3, 7, 8.

    A 3

    B 5

    C 8

    D 6

2 What is the probability of rolling a 3 in a single roll of a die?

    F $\dfrac{1}{3}$

    G $\dfrac{1}{6}$

    H $\dfrac{1}{2}$

    J 1

3 Mary has 3 children. Their ages are 3, 4, and 8 years old. What is the mean of the ages of Mary's children?

    A 2

    B 5

    C 7

    D 15

4 What is the probability of rolling a 9 in a single roll of a die?

    F $\dfrac{1}{3}$

    G 6

    H $\dfrac{1}{2}$

    J 0

5 What is the mean value of this data set: 12, 12, 12, 12?

    A 12

    B 24

    C 6

    D 48

6 What is the probability that a heavy object will fall downward if it is dropped from a height of 3 feet?

    F 0

    G $\dfrac{1}{3}$

    H $\dfrac{1}{2}$

    J 1

7 Five people pick apples at an orchard. They fill a total of 30 crates with apples. What is the mean number of crates of apples each person picks?

    A 6

    B 15

    C 30

    D 150

8 A pet store has 12 kittens. Four of the kittens are black. If one kitten is picked at random, what is the probability that it will be black?

    F $\dfrac{1}{12}$

    G $\dfrac{1}{3}$

    H $\dfrac{1}{4}$

    J 1

9 What is the mean of the numbers 20, 25, and 30?

   A 22

   B 25

   C 29

   D 50

10 At a club party, 100 tickets were sold for a door-prize drawing. Joe bought 1 ticket for the drawing. What is the probability that Joe will win the door prize?

   F 1%

   G 5%

   H 10%

   J 100%

11 A bag contains 5 red marbles, 5 green marbles, and 10 yellow marbles. If you draw a marble at random, what is the probability that it will be red?

   A 5%

   B 10%

   C 25%

   D 50%

12 Tim's test scores were 85, 90, 93, and 88. What was his average score?

   F 80

   G 86

   H 89

   J 94

13 You bought 6 tickets for a raffle drawing. If the total number of tickets sold was 120, what is the probability that you will win the drawing?

   A $\dfrac{1}{120}$

   B $\dfrac{1}{20}$

   C $\dfrac{6}{100}$

   D $\dfrac{5}{6}$

14 There are 8 large cookies in a package. The total weight of the cookies is 16 ounces. What is the mean of the cookies' weight?

   F 1 ounce

   G 2 ounces

   H 4 ounces

   J 16 ounces

15 A letter of the alphabet is chosen at random. There are 26 letters. What is the probability that it is a vowel (a, e, i, o, u)?

   A $\dfrac{1}{5}$

   B $\dfrac{1}{26}$

   C $\dfrac{5}{26}$

   D 1

16 A bus company records how many people ride a particular bus each day. The number of riders was 22, 20, 30, 14, and 24. What was the mean number of riders?

   F 18

   G 22

   H 28

   J 30

Check your answers on pages 120–121.

Lesson 17 Geometric Patterns

Clothing, fabrics, and architecture often have patterns of shapes. The pattern is often what makes them so appealing. The TABE will ask you to study patterns of shapes and complete the missing parts of the patterns.

Example Study this pattern. What would complete the missing part of the pattern?

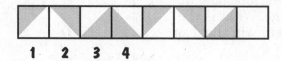

Step 1. Look at the first block in the pattern. Notice how the block is divided on the diagonal.

Step 2. Look at the next block in the pattern. Is it the same as the previous block? How is it different?

Step 3. Continue with the third and fourth blocks. Does the fifth block look like any other block? It looks like the first block. The next block looks like the second block, and the next looks like the third block. The pattern continues every 4 blocks.

The missing block should look like the fourth block, which completes the pattern.

Example Study the pattern of shapes formed by adding blocks. If the pattern continues, how many blocks will be needed to make the next shape?

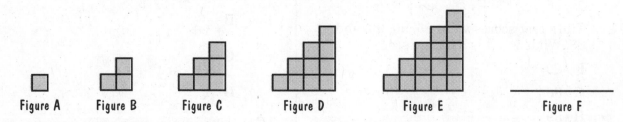

Step 1. Look at figure C. Compare figure C to figure B. Figure C was created by taking figure B and adding a column. How tall is the extra column? It is 1 block taller than the tallest column in figure B.

Step 2. Compare figures C and D. Does the pattern repeat itself from figure C to D? Yes. Figure D looks like figure C with a column added that is 1 block taller than the tallest column in figure C.

Step 3. Look at figures D and E. Does the pattern repeat itself? Yes.

Step 4. The pattern is: the number of blocks added to the next figure is 1 more than the number of blocks in the tallest column. For figure F the pattern is: $1 + 2 + 3 + 4 + 5 + 6 = 21$.

You will need 21 blocks to make the next shape.

Circle the answer.

1 What two figures are missing from this pattern?

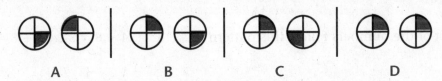

Hint

Look at the relationship between the numbers of blocks in each group to find the pattern.

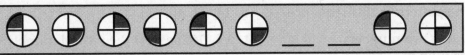

A   B   C   D

1 C The circles for Option C fit in the missing part of the pattern. Option A would not fit the pattern exactly. Options B and D do not fit any of the patterns made by the pairs of circles.

Practice

Read the questions. Circle the answers.

1 Which of these blocks would complete the pattern?

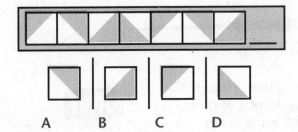

A   B   C   D

2 What two figures are missing from this pattern?

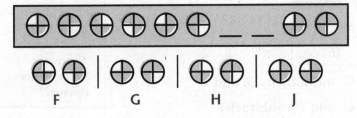

F   G   H   J

Check your answers on page 121.

Functions and Patterns

You don't always have to calculate numbers to answer a math problem. Often you can figure out a math problem by finding a pattern.

Example **What is the pattern in this sequence?** 8, 16, 24, 32, 40, . . .

Step 1. How are the first two numbers related? 16 is 8 more than 8.

Step 2. Decide how the second number (16) is related to the third number (24). 24 + 8 = 16.

Step 3. Decide if the rest of the numbers follow this pattern of "+ 8." (24 + 8 = 32; 32 + 8 = 40)

The pattern is "+ 8."

Example **What are the next three numbers in this sequence?**
3, 2, 5, 4, 7, _____, _____, _____

Step 1. Decide how the first two numbers (3 and 2) are related. 3 − 1 = 2

Decide how the second and third numbers are related. 2 + 3 = 5

Step 2. The pattern is − 1, + 3. Use this pattern to complete the sequence.

7 − 1 = 6, 6 + 3 = 9, 9 − 1 = 8

The next three numbers are 6, 9, and 8.

Test Example

Read the question. Circle the answer.

1   The table shows "Input" numbers that have been changed by a certain rule to get "Output" numbers. Which of these could be the rule for changing the "Input " numbers to "Output "numbers?

Input	Output
1	6
2	11
3	16

A add 7, subtract 2

B multiply by 2, add 10

C multiply by 5, add 1

D add 10, subtract 1

Hint

To find the pattern, ask yourself: "What happens to each number throughout the sequence? Does it increase or decrease? By how much does it change?"

1   C **multiply by 5, add 1** Option A works only for input number 1. Option B only works for input number 3. Option D only works for input number 2.

Read the questions. Circle the answers.

1 Which group of numbers is missing from this number pattern?

18, 21, 24, __, __, __, 36

A 25, 26, 27

B 26, 28, 30

C 27, 30, 33

D 28, 30, 34

2 Which group of numbers is missing from this number pattern?

5, 10, 9, 14, 13, __, __, __

F 12, 11, 10

G 14, 15, 16

H 15, 17, 19

J 18, 17, 22

3 This table shows "Input" numbers that have been changed by a certain rule to get "Output" numbers. Which of these could be the rule?

Input	Output
3	7
2	4
1	1

A add 3, then subtract 2

B add 4, then subtract 2

C multiply by 3, then subtract 2

D multiply by 3, then subtract 3

Rolando recorded his weight every month. This table shows his weight for the first eight months of the year. Read the table. Answer number 4.

January	180
February	175
March	178
April	173
May	176
June	171
July	174
August	169

4 Which of these best describes Rolando's weight loss and gain pattern?

F lose 5, gain 3

G lose 5, gain 5

H lose 3, gain 5

J lose 5, lose 3

Liz is using square tiles to cover her counter. This picture shows two rows of tile on the counter. Study the diagram. Answer number 5.

5 Which of these describes the pattern of the tiles in the two rows?

A 2 dark, 1 light, 2 dark, 1 light

B 2 dark, 2 light, 2 dark, 1 light

C 2 dark, 1 light, 1 dark, 1 light

D 2 dark, 2 light, 1 dark, 1 light

Check your answers on page 121.

Lesson 19 — Expressions and Equations

Sometimes you want to express a quantity in which one value is unknown. An expression is a number phrase in which an unknown value is represented by a letter. For example, the expression, $x + 8$, represents a quantity that is 8 more than an unknown value, x. In this expression, x is called a variable because its value can be any number.

An equation shows the value of an expression: for example, $x + 8 = 15$. According to this equation, if you add 8 to x, the result is 15. On the TABE, you will be asked to solve the equation, that is, find the value of the variable, x.

Example Solve the equation for m: $m + 4 = 9$

Step 1. Find an operation that makes the expression on the left side of the equation equal to the variable.
$$m + 4 - 4 = m$$
Subtracting 4 makes the expression on the left side of the equation equal to m.

Step 2. If you perform the same operation on both sides of the equation, then the equation is still true.
$$m + 4 = 9$$
$$m + 4 - 4 = 9 - 4$$

Step 3. Simplify both sides of the equation.
$$m + 4 - 4 = 9 - 4$$
$$m = 5$$

The value of the variable m in this equation is 5.

Test Example

Read the question. Circle the answer.

1   Solve the equation for x: $3 \times x = 15$

　　A $x = 3$

　　B $x = 5$

　　C $x = 15$

　　D $x = 45$

Hint

Remember that addition and subtraction cancel and multiplication and division cancel.

1   B $x = 5$
By dividing each side of the equation by 3, you find the value of x.
$$3 \times x \div 3 = 15 \div 3 = 5$$

Read the questions. Circle the answers.

1 Solve the equation for x: $x + 6 = 8$

A $x = 8$

B $x = 48$

C $x = 4$

D $x = 2$

2 Solve the equation for y: $y - 5 = 4$

F $y = 9$

G $y = 1$

H $y = 7$

J $y = 3$

3 Solve the equation for h: $6 = h - 3$

A $h = 1$

B $h = 5$

C $h = 3$

D $h = 9$

4 Solve the equation for n: $5 = n + 2$

F $n = 3$

G $n = 4$

H $n = 6$

J $n = 7$

5 Solve the equation for h: $h \times 2 = 14$

A $h = 4$

B $h = 7$

C $h = 3$

D $h = 8$

6 Solve the equation for y: $y \div 3 = 3$

F $y = 9$

G $y = 1$

H $y = 7$

J $y = 3$

7 Solve the equation for m: $m \times 4 = 28$

A $m = 4$

B $m = 7$

C $m = 2$

D $m = 9$

8 Solve the equation for x: $8 = x \div 2$

F $x = 4$

G $x = 8$

H $x = 12$

J $x = 16$

Check your answers on page 121.

Read the questions. Circle the answers.

1 Which group of numbers is missing from the number pattern?

4, 8, 5, 9, 6, __, __, __, 8, 12

A   3, 7, 4

B   10, 7, 11

C   8, 5, 9

D   7, 10, 11

2 What number is missing from this number pattern?

5, 1, 10, 2, 20, 4, __, 8, 80

F   14

G   30

H   40

J   50

Maria has planted tulip bulbs and is recording the growth pattern of the flowers. Study the table, then answer number 3.

DAY	INCHES GROWN
Day 1	1
Day 3	3
Day 5	4
Day 7	6
Day 9	7
Day 11	9
Day 13	10

3 Which of these answers describes the growth pattern of the tulips?

A   Grow 2 inches, grow 1 inch

B   Grow 3 inches, grow 2 inches

C   Grow 1 inch, grow 3 inches

D   Grow 3 inches, grow 4 inches

4 Which group of numbers is missing from this number pattern?

5, 7, 9, 11, __, __, __, 19, 21

F   12, 13, 14

G   13, 15, 17

H   13, 16, 17

J   14, 16, 18

5 What two figures are missing from this pattern?

A   △ ▯

B   △ ▯

C   △ ▮

D   △ ▯

6 What two figures are missing from this pattern?

○ □ △ ○ □ _____ , _____ , □ △

circle, square, triangle, circle, square, _____, _____, square, triangle

F   circle, triangle

G   triangle, circle

H   triangle, square

J   circle, square

7 If $48 \div n = 8$, then n is

   A 6

   B 40

   C 56

   D 384

8 Kevin bought 2 cartons of eggs with 12 eggs in each carton. How many cakes can he bake if each cake needs 4 eggs?

   F 6

   G 8

   H 18

   J 24

9 Theresa volunteers in the monkey house at the zoo. There are 14 monkeys and she feeds each one 5 bananas. How many bananas does she need to feed all the monkeys?

   A 3

   B 9

   C 19

   D 70

10 Adriana bought 3 bags of dog food for each of her 3 dogs. Each bag will provide 8 bowls of food. How many bowls of food does Adriana have for her dogs?

   F 24

   G 14

   H 48

   J 72

11 Solve the equation for x: $x - 5 = 6$

   A $x = 1$

   B $x = 4$

   C $x = 9$

   D $x = 11$

12 Tran needs to buy paper cups for a party. Cups come in packs of 12 and 8. If he buys 3 packs of each, how many cups does Tran have?

   F 20

   G 23

   H 60

   J 96

13 If $24 \times n = 72$, then n is

   A 3

   B 4

   C 48

   D 96

14 Solve the equation for y: $y \times 8 = 48$

   F $y = 6$

   G $y = 1$

   H $y = 7$

   J $y = 3$

Check your answers on pages 121–122.

Lesson 20 Appropriate Units

When you measure the length, width, or height of an object, you will use units of length. There are two sets of units that are often used: standard units and metric units.

Study this list. Then look at the examples.

> 1 foot = 12 inches
> 1 yard = 3 feet = 36 inches
> 1 meter = 100 centimeters
> 1 inch = 2.54 centimeters
> 1 meter ≈ 39.4 inches ≈ 3.28 feet

Test Example

Read the question. Circle the answer.

1 Which of these is a reasonable value for the thickness of a textbook?

  A 3 centimeters

  B 20 centimeters

  C 1 meter

  D 5 meters

Hint

Remember that a centimeter is about $\frac{1}{2}$ inch and that a meter is about 1 yard.

1 **A 3 centimeters** From the list, you can see that 3 centimeters is slightly more than one inch, which is a reasonable thickness for a book. The other measures are much too large.

Read the questions. Circle the answers.

1 About how long is a school bus?

A 20 centimeters

B 100 inches

C 8 feet

D 15 meters

2 Which measure is a good estimate for the length of the word "good" in this sentence?

F 1 centimeter

G 5 inches

H 1 foot

J 1 meter

3 Which of these measures is about the same as 5 meters?

A 5 feet

B 8 feet

C 15 feet

D 100 feet

4 About how high is the ceiling in a typical house?

F 20 inches

G 8 feet

H 1,000 inches

J 6 meters

5 Which is equivalent to a length of 10 inches?

A 2.54 centimeters

B 2.54 meters

C 25.4 feet

D 25.4 centimeters

6 Which of these lengths is greater than 1 yard?

F 10 centimeters

G 30 inches

H 1 meter

J 2 feet

7 Which of these lengths could describe the distance across the front of a standard-sized television?

A 5 centimeters

B 5 inches

C 25 centimeters

D 25 inches

8 Which measure is the best estimate for the width of a two-lane street?

F 10 meters

G 50 centimeters

H 500 feet

J 50 yards

Check your answers on page 122.

In order to determine the length of an object, you measure it with a ruler. Many rulers have two measurement scales. One scale shows distance in inches. The other scale shows distance in centimeters. Line up the ruler so that the zero mark is at one end of the length to be measured and then read the length on the scale.

Each unit on a ruler is broken into smaller parts. There are usually either 8 or 16 lines between each inch mark. These lines represent $\frac{1}{8}$ inch or $\frac{1}{16}$ inch. Centimeters are divided into 10 parts. Each part is $\frac{1}{10}$ centimeter, or 1 millimeter.

Test Example

Read the question. Circle the answer.

1   Use the inch ruler to find the length of the nail.

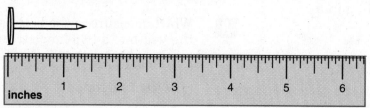

Hint

Be sure to note the measurement scale of the marks because not all rulers are the same.

A   1 inch

B $1\frac{3}{8}$ inch

C $1\frac{3}{4}$ inch

D   2 inch

---

1   B $1\frac{3}{8}$ **inch** The point of the nail matches the sixth line after the

1 inch mark, so the length is $1\frac{6}{16}$ inch $= 1\frac{3}{8}$ inch.

Practice

Read the questions. Circle the answers.

1 What is the length of this rectangle?

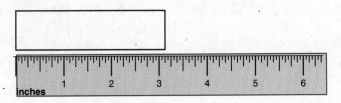

A 3 inches

B $3\frac{1}{16}$ inches

C $3\frac{1}{8}$ inches

D $3\frac{1}{2}$ inches

2 How long is the line below?

F 4.4 centimeters

G $4\frac{1}{2}$ inches

H 4.6 centimeters

J 5 centimeters

3 How long is the line?

A $2\frac{1}{2}$ centimeters

B $2\frac{1}{2}$ inches

C $2\frac{3}{4}$ inches

D 3 inches

4 How long is the paper clip?

F 4.7 centimeters

G $4\frac{1}{2}$ inches

H 5 centimeters

J $4\frac{3}{4}$ inches

Check your answers on page 122.

Lesson 22 · Time

It's 1:00 p.m., and your daughter gets home from school at 3:00 p.m. How much time do you have to go buy groceries before she gets home? You decide that you have 2 hours.

You think about how to use your time every day. On the TABE you will have to solve time problems as well.

Example **Use a clock face to solve some time problems. The movie *Endless Storm* starts at 3:15 p.m. and ends at 5:00 p.m. How long is the movie?**

Step 1. Find the key facts. The start and end times are the important facts you need to know.

Starting time	3:15
Ending time	5:00

Step 2. Count the hours. 3:15 to 4:15 is 1 hour.

Step 3. Count the 5-minute segments starting after 4:15. There are nine 5-minute segments. Multiply: 9 × 5 = 45. Add another 45 minutes to 1 hour.

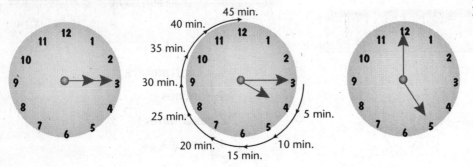

The movie is 1 hour and 45 minutes long.

Test Example

Read the question. Circle the answer.

1 What is the estimated hiking time for the longest route between the Picnic Area and the Entrance?

A 1 hour and 3 minutes

B 1 hour and 14 minutes

C 1 hour and 10 minutes

D 1 hour and 40 minutes

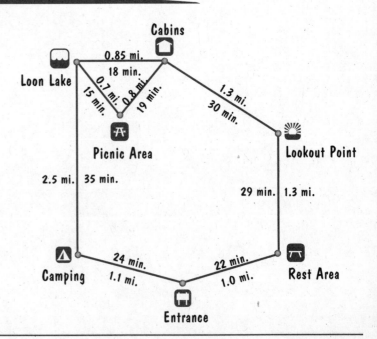

1 D 1 hour and 40 minutes The longer route is from the Picnic Area to Cabins to Lookout Point to Rest Area to Entrance.

Path	Hiking Time	Hiking Time Rounded to the nearest ten
Picnic Area to Cabins	0:19	0:20
Cabins to Lookout Point	0:30	0:30
Lookout Point to Rest Area	0:29	0:30
Rest Area to Entrance	0:22	0:20

Practice

Read the question. Circle the answer.

1 What time will the clock show in 50 minutes?

A 10:50

B 11:20

C 11:30

D 10:30

2 Belinda started driving home from her grandmother's at 9:15 p.m. She arrived home at 11:30 p.m. How long did it take her to drive home?

F 1 hour and 15 minutes

G 2 hours and 15 minutes

H 1 hour and 45 minutes

J 2 hours and 30 minutes

3 Brendan began mowing the Sander's lawn at 7:55 a.m. He finished at 9:15 a.m. How long did it take him to mow the lawn?

A 1 hour and 10 minutes

B 2 hours and 10 minutes

C 1 hour and 20 minutes

D 2 hours and 25 minutes

This map shows the area around the town of Alton including the distance in miles and the driving time between towns. For example, the distance between Stow and Rome is 70 miles and the driving time is 1 hour and 15 minutes. Study the map. Then do numbers 4 and 5.

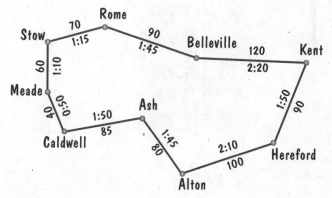

4 What is the estimated driving time for the shortest route between Alton and Belleville?

F 3 hours and 10 minutes

G 6 hours and 20 minutes

H 6 hours and 30 minutes

J 5 hours and 20 minutes

5 What is the estimated driving time for the shortest route between Alton and Meade?

A 4 hours and 45 minutes

B 5 hours and 20 minutes

C 4 hours and 20 minutes

D 4 hours and 25 minutes

Check your answers on page 122.

Lesson 23 Temperature

Thermometers are used to measure indoor and outdoor temperature, body temperature, and also food temperature. On the TABE you will be asked to read the temperature on a thermometer.

Example **This thermometer is hung on the outside of a house. What temperature does the thermometer show?**

Step 1. Look at the shaded part of the thermometer. Find the number at or below the shaded point. On this thermometer, it ends just above 70. The 70 stands for 70°F, or 70 degrees Fahrenheit.

Step 2. Count each line above 70. There are only 4 lines between 70 and 80, so each line stands for 2°F. Count up from 70 by twos for each line.

The temperature on the thermometer shows 74°F.

Test Example

Read the question. Circle the answer.

1 What temperature does the thermometer show?

A 42°F

B 45°F

C 46°F

D 48°F

> **TABE Strategy**
>
> To read the temperature on a thermometer, look at the end point of the shaded part, and then count up from the closest number below it.

1 **C 46°F** Count up 3 lines above 40 to reach 46°F. Option A is one line above 40. Option B is the midpoint between the second and third line. Option D is 4 lines above 40.

Applied Math

Read the question. Circle the answer.

1 What temperature does the thermometer show?

A 20°F

B 22°F

C 25°F

D 28°F

2 What temperature does the thermometer show?

F 70°F

G 72°F

H 75°F

J 78°F

3 George left home at 3:20 and returned at 5:05. How long was he out?

A 1 hour, 25 minutes

B 1 hour, 45 minutes

C 2 hours, 5 minutes

D 2 hours, 25 minutes

4 What temperature does the thermometer show?

F 90°F

G 92°F

H 95°F

J 98°F

5 Jack started a hike at 9:45 a.m. He returned at 11:30 a.m. How long did he hike?

A 1 hour and 15 minutes

B 1 hour and 30 minutes

C 1 hour and 45 minutes

D 2 hours and 25 minutes

6 What temperature does the thermometer show?

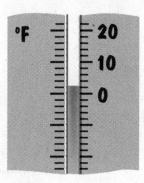

F 0°F

G 2°F

H 12°F

J 22°F

Check your answers on page 122.

Lesson 24 — Length and Distance

How far do you travel when you walk to work or drive to the store? The distance you travel is a measure of length. However, most people do not measure these types of distances in feet or meters. Most distances are measured in units of miles or kilometers. A kilometer is 1,000 meters.

Study this list. Then look at the examples.

> 1 mile = 5,280 feet
> 1 kilometer = 1,000 meters
> 1 mile ≈ 1.6 kilometers
> 1 kilometer ≈ 0.62 mile

Example Mike runs 3 miles everyday at lunchtime. How many kilometers does he run?

Step 1. Decide what number you need to multiply to change from miles to kilometers. Each mile is 1.6 kilometers.

Step 2. Convert from one measurement to the other.

3 miles = 3 × 1.6 kilometers = 4.8 kilometers

Step 3. Check your answer to be sure it is reasonable.

Each mile is slightly more than $1\frac{1}{2}$ kilometers so he runs more kilometers than miles. The answer is reasonable.

Test Example

Read the question. Circle the answer.

1 A nearby city is 3,000 meters away. What is that distance in kilometers?

    A 3 kilometers

    B 30 kilometers

    C 1,000 kilometers

    D 3,000 kilometers

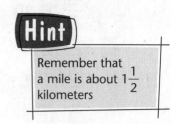

Hint

Remember that a mile is about $1\frac{1}{2}$ kilometers

1 A 3 kilometers Each kilometer is equal to 1,000 meters so you find the number of kilometers by dividing 3,000 meters by 1,000. Answer B is the result of division by 100. Answers C and D are too large to be correct.

Read the questions. Circle the answers.

1 About how long is a 10 kilometer race?

A 3 miles

B 6 miles

C 10 miles

D 16 miles

2 What is a good estimate of the distance from New York to Los Angeles?

F 100 kilometers

G 500 kilometers

H 5,000 kilometers

J 50,000 kilometers

3 Which of these measures is the same as 3 miles?

A 5,280 feet

B 10,560 feet

C 15,840 feet

D 21,120 feet

4 An airliner travels at a height of about 32,000 feet. About how far above the ground is the plane?

F 1 mile

G 2 miles

H 6 miles

J 60 miles

5 Which distance is the longest?

A 10,000 feet

B 100 miles

C 100 kilometers

D 10,000 meters

6 A road sign says that you are 50 kilometers from your destination. How many miles do you need to travel?

F 11 miles

G 31 miles

H 80 miles

J 100 miles

7 Which distance is about the same distance as 200 miles?

A 32 kilometers

B 120 kilometers

C 320 kilometers

D 750 kilometers

8 About how far could you travel in an hour by walking quickly?

F 100 meters

G 7 kilometers

H 45 kilometers

J 175 kilometers

Check your answers on page 122.

To find the perimeter of something means to measure the boundary around it. Look at this diagram of a yard. The perimeter is the distance around the yard.

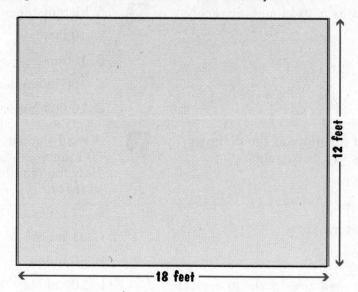

Example **What is the perimeter of the yard shown in the diagram above?**

Step 1. Use the measurements on the diagram. The yard is 12 feet long by 18 feet wide. Not all of the sides are marked, but the unmarked sides match the marked sides, so you know that the opposite sides are equal in length.

Step 2. Add all four sides to find the perimeter of the yard: 12 + 12 + 18 + 18 = 60.

The perimeter of the yard is 60 feet.

Example **What is the perimeter of the yard as shown in the diagram below?**

Step 1. Look at the measurements. The top and right borders don't look equal to the bottom and left borders.

Step 2. If you draw two lines to "close up" the square, you'll see that all the sides are equal. Add all the sides: 7 + 7 + 7 + 7 = 28.

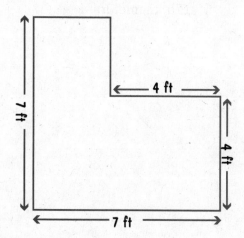

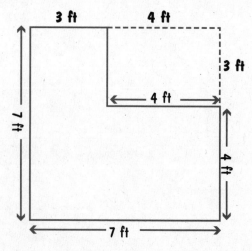

The perimeter of the yard is 28 feet.

Lou is planning a vegetable garden. His diagram shows the dimensions of the garden. Study the diagram and then answer the question.

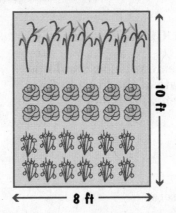
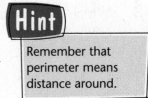

1 What is the perimeter of the garden?

A 18 feet

B 36 feet

C 78 feet

D 80 feet

---

1 **B 36 feet** 8 ft. × 2 = 16 ft; 10 ft. × 2 = 20 ft;
16 ft. + 20 ft. = 36 ft. Option A added only two sides (8 + 10);
Option C multiplied the two sides, then subtracted 2. Option D
multiplied the two sides.

Hint

Remember that perimeter means distance around.

Practice

Study the diagram. Then answer number 1.

24 inches

← 18 inches →

Read the question. Circle the answer.

1 A metal frame will go around the perimeter of the poster. How much framing will be needed for this poster?

A 42 inches

B 72 inches

C 84 inches

D 96 inches

TABE Strategy

Study the diagram carefully. Then read the question. Look for words and numbers in the question that may tell you what to look for in the diagram.

2 A garden plot in the shape of a square measures 5 feet on each side. What is the perimeter of the plot?

F 5 feet

G 10 feet

H 20 feet

J 25 feet

Check your answers on page 122.

Read the questions. Circle the answers.

1 Which measurement below would be the best estimate of the height of a standard door in your home?

A 1 yard

B 2 meters

C 15 feet

D 10 centimeters

2 Which of these measurements is the same as 12 feet?

F 72 inches

G 120 inches

H 2 yards

J 4 yards

3 Which of these measurements is about the same as 100 inches?

A 40 centimeters

B 250 centimeters

C 5 meters

D 30 meters

4 An airplane is scheduled to leave one city at 10:35 a.m. and arrive at another city at 12:15 p.m. How long is the scheduled flight?

F 1 hour and 20 minutes

G 1 hour and 40 minutes

H 2 hours and 20 minutes

J 2 hours and 45 minutes

5 Bill made a cake for his daughter's birthday. The recipe says the cake should bake for 55 minutes and then cool for 10 minutes before being removed from the pan. If he puts the cake in the oven at 1:00, when will the cake be ready to remove from the pan?

A 1:10

B 1:55

C 2:05

D 2:55

6 Libby is leaving work at 7:30 p.m. The last train leaves at 8:25 p.m. How much time will she have to get to the train station?

F 35 minutes

G 55 minutes

H 1 hour and 25 minutes

J 1 hour and 55 minutes

7 What temperature does the thermometer show?

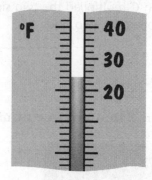

A 24°F

B 26°F

C 28°F

D 29°F

8 What temperature does the thermometer show?

F 82°F

G 84°F

H 88°F

J 89°F

9   How long is the rectangle below?

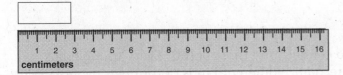

A $2\frac{3}{4}$ inches

B 2.8 centimeters

C 3 centimeters

D 2.5 centimeters

Study the diagram. Then answer numbers 10 and 11.

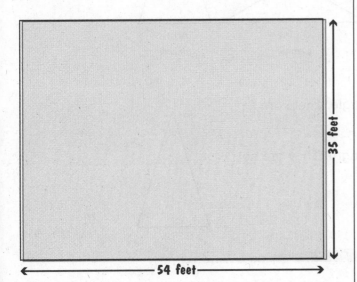

10   Lian is putting a fence around her yard for her dog. How much fencing will she need to buy?

F 70 feet

G 89 feet

H 108 feet

J 178 feet

11   If Lian extended each side by one foot, what would the perimeter of the fence be?

A 76 feet

B 180 feet

C 182 feet

D 190 feet

12   Rick decided to run in a marathon, which is slightly more than 26 miles long. About how many kilometers will he run?

F 4 kilometers

G 10 kilometers

H 41 kilometers

J 150 kilometers

13   Which of these measures is closest to the length of your thumb?

A 1 centimeter

B 1 inch

C 7 centimeters

D 20 inches

14   What speed is about the same as the speed of a car traveling 60 miles per hour on the highway?

F 10 kilometers per hour

G 36 kilometers per hour

H 100 kilometers per hour

J 500 kilometers per hour

Check your answers on pages 122–123.

Lesson 26 Triangles

You can build a triangle by drawing lines to connect any three points. Every triangle has exactly three sides and three angles. You can recognize different kinds of triangles by looking at the angles.

In an equilateral triangle, all of the angles are the same and all of the sides have the same length. A right triangle has one angle that is 90° (like the corner of a square). An obtuse triangle has one angle that is greater than 90°. In an acute triangle, all of the angles are less than 90°. An equilateral triangle is also an acute triangle.

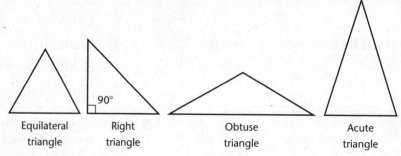

| Equilateral triangle | Right triangle | Obtuse triangle | Acute triangle |

Example What kind of triangle is shown?

Step 1. Look for a right angle or an obtuse angle. There are none so this is an acute triangle.

Step 2. Decide if all the sides are the same length. They are not the same so this is not an equilateral triangle.

It is an acute triangle.

Test Example

Study the triangle. Circle the answer.

1 What kind of triangle is this?

   A acute triangle

   B equilateral

   C obtuse triangle

   D right triangle

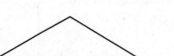

Hint

Every triangle has at least two acute angles. Look at the third angle to find the kind of triangle.

---

1 C obtuse triangle
The triangle has one angle that is greater than 90°.
It is an obtuse triangle.

1 How many angles does a triangle have?

A 1

C 3

B 2

D 4

2 What kind of triangle is shown?

F acute triangle

G equilateral triangle

H right triangle

J obtuse triangle

3 Which statement describes an equilateral triangle?

A two sides are the same length

B one obtuse angle and two acute angles

C three angles are the same

D all sides have different lengths

4 The dashed line divides the square into two triangles. What kind of triangles are they?

F acute triangles

G equilateral triangles

H right triangles

J obtuse triangles

5 Which of these shapes is a triangle?

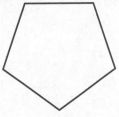   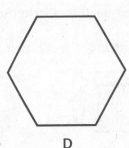

A   B   C   D

6 Which of these shapes is a triangle?

 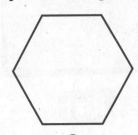  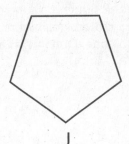

F   G   H   J

Check your answers on page 123.

Lesson 27 Solid Figures

Many solid figures have shapes that you can recognize and label. For example, a ball is a sphere, a can is a cylinder, and sugar sometimes comes in a cube.

On the TABE, you will be asked to identify solid figures that are similar to those you see every day.

Example **What type of solid figure is the ice you usually see in a glass of water?**

Solid figures have particular attributes. Read the descriptions below:

Sphere	**Cone**	**Cylinder**	**Cube**
A 3-dimensional figure that is round and circular	A 3-dimensional figure that has a flat, round base and pointed top	A 3-dimensional figure that has a flat, round base and top and curved side	A 3-dimensional figure that has 6 flat, square sides

Strategy. What are the attributes of a typical piece of ice? It has 6 square sides that are flat.

The ice is usually in the shape of a cube.

Test Example

Read the question. Circle the answer.

1 Which of the following solid figures is a sphere?

    A   B   C   D

1 **B** This figure is a sphere because it is a round circular, 3-dimensional figure. Option A is a cube. Option C is a cone. Option D is a cylinder.

Hint

It doesn't matter what position a shape is in, it is still the same shape. For example, an ice-cream cone, although upside-down, is still a cone.

Read the questions. Circle the answers.

1 What is the name of the following figure?

A cube

B cylinder

C cone

D sphere

2 What is the name of this solid figure?

F sphere

G cone

H cube

J cylinder

3 What is the shape of the box of tissues?

A sphere

B cone

C cube

D cylinder

4 Which of the following solid figures is a cylinder?

F   G   H   J

5 Which of the following figures is <u>not</u> named correctly?

circle   cone   cylinder   cube
A   B   C   D

6 Which of the following is <u>not</u> a solid figure?

F   G   H   J

Check your answers on page 123.

Lesson 28 Symmetry

Picture a sunflower. If you could draw a line directly down the center of the flower, you would see that both sides are identical. This is an example of symmetry. Symmetry means that two halves look exactly the same. If you look around, you'll see many other examples of symmetry in nature and in man-made objects. On the TABE, you will be asked to identify two symmetrical halves.

Example Look at the building in the drawing. Where would you draw a line to divide the building into symmetrical halves?

Step 1. Look at the horizontal line across the building. Are the two halves symmetrical? Do the parts in each half match? No, the top and bottom of the building do not match, so this line does not divide the building into symmetrical halves.

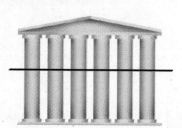

Step 2. Look at the vertical line that divides the building into two halves. Do the parts in each half match? Yes.

A vertical line down the middle of the building would divide it into symmetrical halves.

Text Example

This diagram shows a plan for a park. Study the diagram. Then answer the question.

1   Which of these lines divides the park into symmetrical halves?

    A   Line A

    B   Line B

    C   Line C

    D   Line D

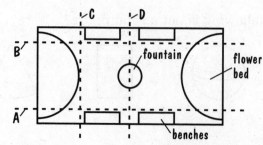

1 **D** **Line D** divides the diagram into symmetrical halves with identical parts. Option A and Option B divide the diagram into top and bottom sections that are not symmetrical. Option C divides the diagram vertically into sections that are not symmetrical.

Practice

This diagram shows the dimensions of a tennis court. Study the diagram. Then do numbers 1 through 4.

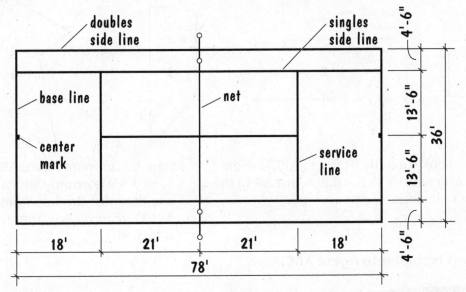

1 What divides the tennis court into symmetrical halves?

A Base line

B Doubles side line

C Singles side line

D Net

2 What is the perimeter of the tennis court?

F 114 feet H 228 feet

G 144 feet J 312 feet

3 Which of these measurements is about the same as the width of the tennis court?

A 8 yards

B 18 yards

C 4 meters

D 12 meters

4 If a player walked from the center mark to the net and back to the base line, how many feet did she walk?

F 36 feet H 78 feet

G 39 feet J 156 feet

TABE **Strategy**

If you could cut out the diagram and fold it in half, which way would you fold it so that both sides matched?

Check your answers on page 123.

You notice that someone you work with has the same shoes you do. Your co-worker's shoes are a different size than yours but are the same in every other way. You would say that your shoes are similar. Shapes can be similar as well. On the TABE you will be asked to compare different shapes and determine if they are similar.

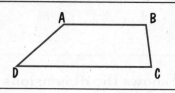

Example Which figure is similar to figure ABCD?

 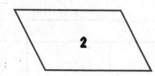  

Step 1. Look carefully at figure ABCD. Note the characteristics of the figure including the angles and sides.

Step 2. Compare figure ABCD to figures 1, 2, 3, and 4. Determine which of these figures has the most similar characteristics to figure ABCD, regardless of the size or how the figure is turned.

Figure 3 is similar to figure ABCD.

Test Example

Read the question. Circle the answer.

1 Which of these figures are similar to figure XYZ?

A figures 1 and 4

B figures 3 and 5

C figures 2 and 4

D figures 3 and 4

TABE Strategy

Mentally try to place figure XYZ over each answer choice. If the outlines of the shapes line up, the figures are similar.

1 **D figures 3 and 4** These figures have similar characteristics to figure XYZ. If you look closely at the angles and the sides of XYZ, you will notice that figures 3 and 4 match up. The only differences are the size and which way they are turned. Options A, B, and D include only 1 figure that is similar to XYZ.

Read the questions. Circle the answers.

1 Which of these figures is similar to figure X?

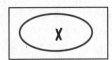

A figures 1 and 5

B figures 2 and 3

C figure 3 only

D figure 4 only

2 Which of these figures are similar to figure ABCDE?

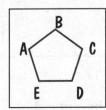

F figures 1 and 2

G figures 2 and 3

H figures 2 and 4

J figures 1 and 4

3 Which of these figures are similar to ABCD?

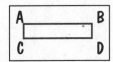

A figures 1 and 5

B figures 1 and 4

C figures 2 and 3

D figures 2 and 4

Check your answers on page 123.

Lesson 30 Congruence

Congruent shapes are two figures that are exactly the same in shape and size. Find out if two figures are congruent by placing one over the other. If they match exactly, the figures are congruent. If you cannot move the figures around, try to imagine whether the figures would fit one on top of the other exactly.

Example **Which set of shapes is congruent?**

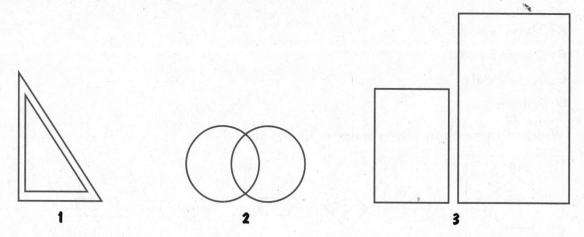

1   2   3

Step 1. Look for sets of the same shape. Although Set 3 is 2 rectangles, they are not shaped the same. Cross out that set.

Step 2. Of the sets with the same shape, look for shapes that are exactly the same size. Set 1 has the same shapes, but they are not the same size. Cross out that set.

The circles in set 2 are congruent because they are exactly the same shape and size.

Test Example

Read the question. Circle the answer.

1   Which parts of the figure are congruent?

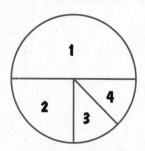

A   1 and 2   C   2 and 4

B   2 and 3   D   3 and 4

1   **D 3 and 4** These parts are congruent because they are the same shape and size. They would match perfectly when placed on top of one another. Options A, B and C show two shapes that are not exactly the same.

Read the questions. Circle the answers.

1 Which shapes in the figure are congruent?

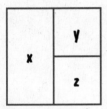

A 1 and 2

B 3 and 4

C 1 and 3

D 2 and 4

2 Which parts of the figure are congruent?

F x and y

G x and z

H y and z

G x, y, and z

3 Which figures are congruent?

A 1 and 2

B 2 and 3

C 3 and 4

D 1 and 4

4 Which figures are congruent?

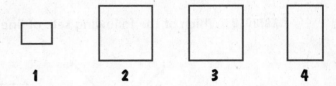

F figures 1 and 2

G figures 2 and 3

H figures 3 and 1

J figures 4 and 2

5 Which figures are congruent?

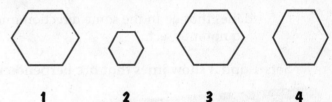

A 1 and 2

B 2 and 3

C 3 and 4

D 1 and 3

Hint

Remember that congruency means that two shapes are matching at *all* parts when placed on top of one another.

Check your answers on pages 123–124.

Lesson 31 | Parallel and Perpendicular

If two lines never cross one another, they are parallel lines. If two lines cross one another and make a 90° angle, they are perpendicular lines. Many street intersections are two streets that make perpendicular lines.

Example Which of the following sets of lines are perpendicular?

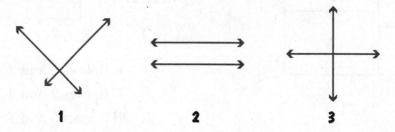

Strategy. Look at each set of lines and decide if the two lines cross at a 90° angle.

- If the lines in any of the sets make a 90° angle, they are perpendicular.

- Lines that go in the same direction and do not touch are parallel lines. Parallel lines do not intersect.

Sets 1 and 3 show lines that are perpendicular.

Test Example

Read the question. Circle the answer.

1   Which picture show lines that are perpendicular to one another?

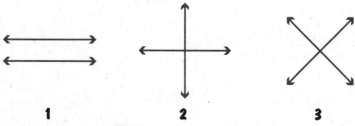

   A   picture 2 only

   B   picture 3 only

   C   pictures 1 and 2 only

   D   pictures 2 and 3 only

TABE Strategy

The key word *only* in the options is a clue that there may be more than one answer. Remember to read all options before choosing one.

1   **D   pictures 2 and 3 only** Both pictures numbered 2 and 3 show lines that cross at a 90° angle and are therefore perpendicular lines. Options A and B do not name both pictures that have perpendicular lines. Option C includes set number 1, which shows parallel lines.

Read the questions. Circle the answers.

1 Which of the following show parallel lines?

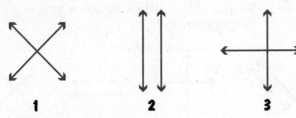

A picture 1 only

B picture 2 only

C pictures 1 and 3 only

D pictures 2 and 3 only

2 Which of these pictures show perpendicular lines?

F picture 1 only

G picture 2 only

H pictures 1 and 3 only

J pictures 2 and 3 only

3 Which of these letters has parallel vertical sides?

A Letter H

B Letter D

C Letter B

D Letters H and D

Look at the diagram below, then answer number 4 and 5.

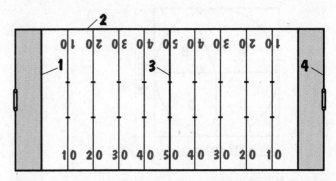

4 Which line on the football field divides the field into symmetrical halves?

F 1

G 2

H 3

J 4

5 How are the two 40 yard lines on a football field related to one another?

A parallel

B perpendicular

C neither parallel nor perpendicular

D both parallel and perpendicular

Check your answers on page 124.

Study the diagram. Then do numbers 1 and 2.

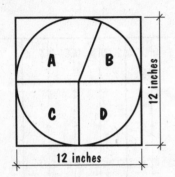

12 inches

12 inches

1 Which of these measurements is equal to the perimeter of the box around the circle?

A 12 inches

B 144 inches

C 4 feet

D 3 yards

2 Which two parts of the circle are congruent?

F parts A and B

G parts B and D

H parts A and D

J parts C and D

3 Jessica went to a movie at 1:00 p.m. this afternoon. The movie ended at 2:50 p.m. How long did the movie last?

A 1 hour and 50 minutes

B 2 hours and 10 minutes

C 2 hours and 50 minutes

D 0 hours and 50 minutes

4 Which of these figures shows a line of symmetry?

1   2   3   4

F 1   **H** 3

G 2   **J** 4

Read the questions. Circle the answers.

5 Which of the following lines are perpendicular?

1   2   3   4

A sets 1 and 2

B sets 2 and 3

C sets 1 and 4

D sets 2 and 4

6 Which line creates a line of symmetry in this triangle?

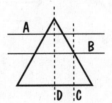

F line A

G line B

H line C

J line D

7 Which of these solid figures is not named correctly?

cube sphere cylinder cone

A cube

B sphere

C cylinder

D cone

8 What two figures are missing from this pattern?

△ ◫ △ ◫ △ ◫ _ _ △ ◫

F △ ◫

G ▲ ◫

H △ ◫

J △ ◫

9 Which of the following figures has a line of symmetry?

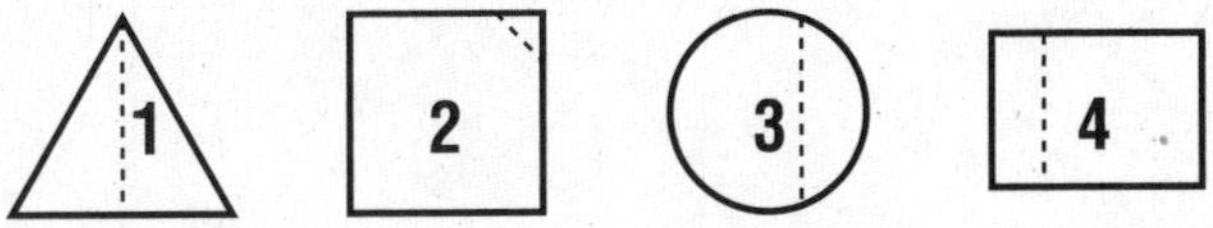

△1 ☐2 ◯3 ☐4

A figure 1

B figure 2

C figure 3

D figure 4

10 Which distance is about the same as 1 kilometer?

F 100 meters

G 1,000 feet

H 1,000 yards

J 2 miles

11 What two figures are missing from this pattern?

◯ ☐ △ ◯ ☐ _____, _____, ☐ △

circle, square, triangle, circle, square, _____, _____, square, triangle

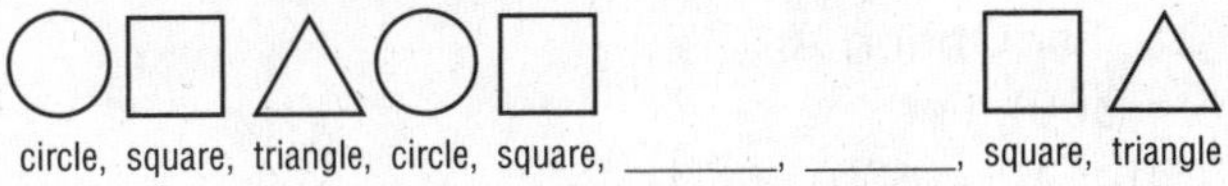

A circle, triangle

B triangle, circle

C triangle, square

D circle, square

12 Which measurement below is exactly the same as 2 yards?

F 2 meters

G 200 centimeters

H 10 feet

J 72 inches

13 Which of the following figures are similar to the figure in the box?

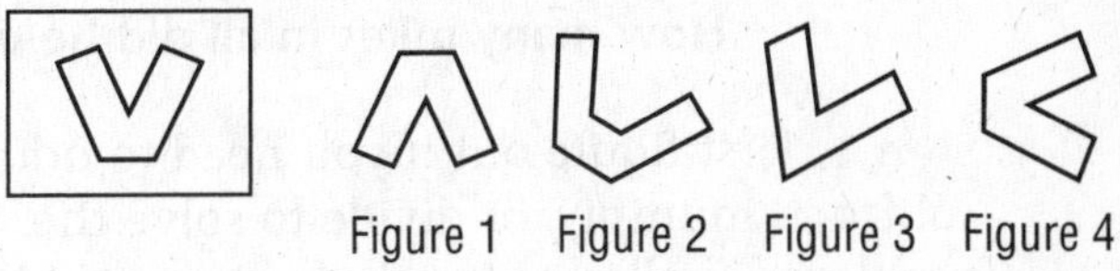

V   Λ   L   L   ＜

Figure 1 Figure 2 Figure 3 Figure 4

A figures 1 and 2

B figures 2 and 3

C figures 3 and 4

D figures 1 and 4

14 What is the perimeter of the rectangle below?

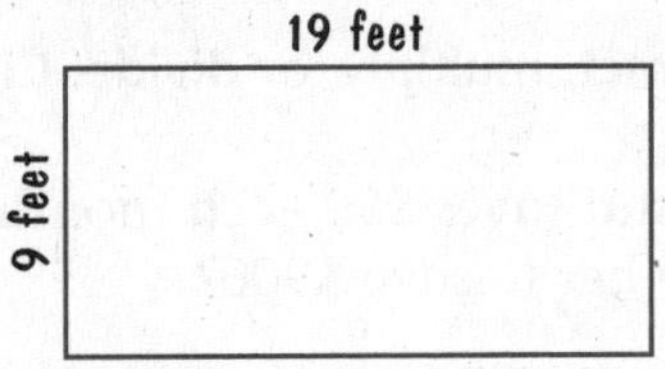

19 feet
9 feet

F 10 feet

G 28 feet

H 56 feet

J 171 feet

Check your answers on page 124.

Lesson 32 Whole Numbers in Context

When driving to a relative's house, you keep track of the distance. You look at the mileage on your car before you begin your trip. It is 78,000. When you arrive, you check the miles on your car. It is now 78,250. You have driven exactly 250 miles. The number is a whole number. On the TABE, you will solve problems in which you calculate whole numbers of miles, feet, or months.

Example Michael kept a record of miles he drove for a week. Tuesday he drove 135 miles. Wednesday he drove 167 miles and Friday he drove 230 miles. How many miles in all did he drive during the week?

Step 1. First figure out if you need to add, subtract, multiply, or divide to solve the problem. *In all* is a clue that you need to add.

Step 2. Add all the numbers.
135 + 167 + 230 = 532

Step 3. Make sure your solution truly answers the question. If it does not, try using another operation.

Michael drove 532 miles.

Test Example

Add, subtract, multiply, or divide. Circle the answer.

1 Crystal saves $50 each month. How many months will it take her to save $900?

  A 6 months

  B 12 months

  C 18 months

  D 24 months

1 .**C 18 months** The goal amount of $900 is divided by the amount she saves each month: 900 ÷ 50 = 18. For Option A, Crystal would have saved only $300 (50 × 6 = 300). For Option B, she would have saved only $600 (50 × 12 = 600). For Option D, the total amount saved would be $1,200 (50 × 24 = 1,200).

Hint

Look for key words that will help you decide how to solve a problem. For example, the word *each* means that the number is the same every time. This often signals multiplication.

Practice

Read the questions. Circle the answers.

1 Kate wanted to know how much exercise she gets at work. She measured the distance to and from the copy machine. The copy machine is 40 feet away. She walks to the copy machine and returns to her desk 7 times every day. How many feet does she walk to use the copier each day?

A 26 feet

B 54 feet

C 280 feet

D 560 feet

2 The Fernandez family took a trip to Springfield, which is 70 miles from their home. Then they traveled from Springfield to New Lenox, which is another 122 miles away. They took the same route back home. How many miles did they travel in all?

F 192 miles

G 244 miles

H 384 miles

J 454 miles

3 Darryl has a car payment of $225 per month. He has a balance of $1350 on his car loan. How many more months does he have to make car payments?

A 6 months

B 9 months

C 12 months

D 24 months

4 Tara saves $40 a month. How many months will it take her to save $800?

F 10 months

G 20 months

H 30 months

J 40 months

5

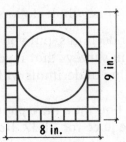

What is the perimeter of the border?

A 8 inches

B 9 inches

C 17 inches

D 34 inches

6 Ray walked to each corner in a big square yard. The distance from each corner to the next is 90 feet. If he starts in one corner and goes all around, what is the total distance he walks?

90 feet

F 180 feet

G 240 feet

H 360 feet

J 450 feet

7

If the perimeter of this figure is 72 centimeters, how long is each side?

A 6 centimeters

B 9 centimeters

C 12 centimeters

D 24 centimeters

Check your answers on page 124–125.

Decimals in Context

When you buy something, you are using decimals. When you pay $39.95 for an item, you are paying thirty-nine whole dollars and $\frac{95}{100}$ of one dollar. Money amounts are the most common uses for decimals, but you also see decimals in temperatures (98.7 is a normal body temperature) or in surveys that report opinions ("50.6% of the moviegoers liked the movie"). Your understanding of decimals will be tested on the TABE.

Example Tonya bought a newspaper for $1.25, milk for $2.75, chips for $0.75, and orange juice for $1.37. How much did Tonya pay for all the items?

Step 1. Decide if you need to add, subtract, multiply, or divide to solve the problem. You need to find out what Tonya paid for **all** the items, so add the numbers. To add numbers with decimals, line up the decimals. Write a decimal point in the answer line under the other decimal points.

$$\begin{array}{r} \$1.25 \\ \$2.75 \\ \$0.75 \\ + \$1.37 \\ \hline . \end{array}$$

Step 2. Adding decimals is like adding whole numbers. Begin adding the numbers in the right-hand column and regroup as necessary. 0.22 = 22 hundredths, or 2 tenths and 2 hundredths. Write 2 in the answer line, and regroup by adding the 2 tenths to next column, the tenths column.

$$\begin{array}{r} 2 \\ \$1.25 \\ \$2.75 \\ \$0.75 \\ + \$1.37 \\ \hline .\ 2 \end{array}$$

Step 3. Now add all the numbers in the tenths column, including the 2 you just regrouped. 2.1 = 21 tenths or "2 and 1 tenth." Write 1 in the answer line, and regroup by adding the 2 to the ones column.

$$\begin{array}{r} 2\ 2 \\ \$1.25 \\ \$2.75 \\ \$0.75 \\ + \$1.37 \\ \hline .12 \end{array}$$

Step 4. Now add the whole numbers, including the 2 you regrouped in the ones column.

$$\begin{array}{r} 2\ 2 \\ \$1.25 \\ \$2.75 \\ \$0.75 \\ + \$1.37 \\ \hline 6.12 \end{array}$$

Tonya paid $6.12 for all the items.

Test Example

Read the question. Circle the answer.

1 Sara wrote a check for $78.85. Before she wrote the check, her balance was $239.75. What is her new balance?

   A $160.10   C $161.10

   B $160.90   D $161.90

Hint

As you add or subtract, remember to regroup, if necessary.

1 **B $160.90** Subtract $78.85 from $239.75. In option A, the numbers in the tenths place were incorrectly subtracted: 0.8 was subtracted from 0.7. In option C, 0.8 was subtracted from 0.7 and the whole dollar amount $239 should have been changed to $238. In option D, the whole dollar amount was not changed when it was subtracted.

Practice

Read the questions. Circle the answers.

1 Melissa bought the following items at the store: a carton of milk for $2.36, a loaf of bread for $1.25, and a jar of peanut butter for $1.67. What was the bill for all the items?

A $4.28

B $5.18

C $5.28

D $6.28

2 Mai's daughter has a temperature of 101.3 degrees. How many degrees above the normal 98.6 degrees is her daughter's temperature?

F 2.7 degrees

G 3.3 degrees

H 3.7 degrees

J 13.7 degrees

3 Mark buys three pens at $1.25 each. How much do the pens cost all together?

A $3.65

B $3.75

C $4.75

D $4.65

4 John wrote a check for $25.01. His checkbook balance was $127.00 before he wrote the check. What is the balance after writing the check?

F $101.01

G $101.99

H $102.99

J $152.01

5 At the beginning of a drive to the store, Anya's odometer read 345.8 miles. When she reached the store, it read 349.2 miles. What distance did Anya drive to get to the store?

A 3.4 miles

B 3.6 miles

C 4.6 miles

D 5.2 miles

6 Dave travels to and from work 35 miles each way. How many miles does he travel in 5 days?

F 40 miles

G 175 miles

H 350 miles

J 700 miles

7 The distance from the edge of this circle to its center is 5 inches. One inch is about 2.5 centimeters. Which measure below is about the same as 5 inches?

A 2 centimeters

B 7.5 centimeters

C 9 centimeters

D 12.5 centimeters

Check your answers on page 125.

Lesson 34 Fractions in Context

When cooking, recipes often specify ingredients using fractions, such as $1\frac{3}{4}$ cups or $\frac{2}{3}$ of a teaspoon. If you ever have to double a recipe, you'll have to be able to add fractions, such as $1\frac{3}{4}$ cups plus $1\frac{3}{4}$ cups to get $3\frac{1}{2}$ cups.

Example **If you need to double $2\frac{2}{3}$ cups of sugar in a recipe, how many cups of sugar should you use?**

Step 1. Decide if you should add, subtract, multiply, or divide. The amount of sugar has to be doubled, so add $2\frac{2}{3} + 2\frac{2}{3}$.

Step 2. Add the fractions first.

$$\begin{array}{r} 2\dfrac{2}{3} \\ +\,2\dfrac{2}{3} \\ \hline \dfrac{4}{3} \end{array}$$

Step 3. You must change $\frac{4}{3}$ to a mixed number since 4 is greater than 3. A mixed number is a whole number and a fraction. Subtract 3 from 4 to make a whole number $(4 - 3 = 1)$. The part left over (1) remains a fraction $\left(\frac{1}{3}\right)$.

$$\frac{4}{3} = 1\frac{1}{3}$$

Step 4. Now add the whole numbers, including the whole number (1) from the mixed number in step 2. $(2 + 2 + 1 = 5)$.

$$\begin{array}{r} 2 \\ +\,2 \\ \hline 4 + 1\dfrac{1}{3} \end{array}$$

Step 5. Add the whole number total to the fraction total $\left(5 + \frac{1}{3} = 5\frac{1}{3}\right)$.

$$2\frac{2}{3} \text{ cups} + 2\frac{2}{3} \text{ cups} = 5\frac{1}{3} \text{ cups.}$$

Test Example

Read the question. Circle the answer.

1   If $2\frac{3}{4}$ cups of flour and $1\frac{1}{4}$ cups of sugar are mixed together, how many cups will the mixture be?

A $3\frac{1}{4}$

B $3\frac{3}{4}$

C 3

D 4

Hint

If the top number and the bottom number are the same $\left(\frac{4}{4}\right)$, it equals 1 whole.

1 D 4 $2\frac{3}{4} + 1\frac{1}{4} = 3\frac{4}{4}$; $\frac{4}{4}$ is equal to 1, so $1 + 3 = 4$. Option A adds the whole numbers correctly, but only includes the fraction $\frac{1}{4}$. Option B adds the whole numbers correctly, but only includes the fraction $\frac{3}{4}$. Option C does not include the fractions in either number.

Practice

Read the questions. Circle the answers.

1 Carlos needs $2\frac{2}{3}$ feet of wire plus another $1\frac{2}{3}$ feet to install his cable television. How many feet of wire does he need?

A 3   C $4\frac{1}{3}$

B 4   D $4\frac{2}{3}$

2 Eva is measuring vanilla to add to a cookie mixture. She adds $\frac{1}{4}$ teaspoon and then $\frac{3}{4}$ teaspoon. How many teaspoons did she add?

F 1   H $1\frac{3}{4}$

G $1\frac{1}{4}$ J 2

3 Kim doubled a recipe for cookies. Instead of $1\frac{1}{4}$ cups of flour, how many cups did she add?

A 2   C $2\frac{1}{2}$

B $2\frac{1}{4}$ D 3

4 Marcia's daughter grew $3\frac{2}{3}$ inches in one year, and $2\frac{2}{3}$ inches the next. How many inches did she grow in these two years?

F 5   H 6

G $5\frac{2}{3}$ J $6\frac{1}{3}$

5 Dane bought 2 CDs for $15.99 each and another CD for $12.99. How much did he spend?

A $34.97

B $42.77

C $44.77

D $44.97

6 Felipe filled the gas tank of his car with $17.45 worth of gas. He gave the cashier $20.00 to pay for the gas. How much change did he get?

F $2.55

G $2.45

H $3.55

J $13.45

7 Rasheed saves $60 every month. How much will he save in 9 months?

A $69

B $180

C $360

D $540

8 Jana has a debt of $1,400 that she wants to pay in monthly installments of $70. How many months will it take for Jana to repay the loan?

A 10 months

B 20 months

C 30 months

D 40 months

Check your answers on page 125.

Read the questions. Circle the answers.

1 Darnell is keeping track of the hours of overtime he worked over the year. He worked 103 hours of overtime in the first 4 months and 127 hours in the next 4 months. He worked 102 hours of overtime in the final months of the year. How many hours of overtime did Darnell work in all?

A 205

B 332

C 340

D 416

2 Luis bought a sweater for $39.98. He gave the cashier a $50 bill. How much change did Luis receive?

F $10.02

G $11.02

H $10.12

J $11.12

3 Chiang is saving $60 a month for a vacation. She needs to save $540 dollars. How long will it take her to save enough for her vacation?

A 6 months

B 9 months

C 12 months

D 18 months

4 You need to double the amount of milk in a recipe. If you double $1\frac{1}{4}$ cups of milk, what amount of milk do you use?

F 2 cups

G $2\frac{1}{4}$ cups

H $2\frac{1}{2}$ cups

J 3 cups

5 If $1\frac{1}{4}$ cups of sugar and $1\frac{3}{4}$ cups of flour are mixed together, how many cups will the mixture be?

A 2

B $2\frac{3}{4}$

C 3

D $3\frac{1}{4}$

6 A basketball court is 94 feet long. If a player runs from one end and back twice, how many feet does she run?

F 94 feet

G 188 feet

H 282 feet

J 376 feet

7 Lin has 180 flower bulbs and wants to plant an equal number next to all four sides of his house. How many bulbs should he plant on each side?

A 45

B 90

C 176

D 720

8 Greg bought the following items at the drug store: toothpaste $1.29; toothbrush $1.99; cold medicine $3.59; and tissues $1.85. How much did he pay for all of the items?

F $6.42

G $6.72

H $8.72

J $9.72

9 Guy bought $4\frac{2}{3}$ feet of fencing, and then he realized he needed another $2\frac{2}{3}$ feet of it. How many feet of fencing did he buy in all?

A 6 feet

B 7 feet

C $7\frac{1}{3}$ feet

D $8\frac{1}{3}$ feet

10 Anna saves $75 every month. How much will she save in 16 months?

F $91

G $450

H $900

J $1,200

11 Joe drove 232 miles from his home to Wellville. From there he drove another 312 miles to Hapsburg. He took the same route home. How many miles did he drive?

A 80 miles

B 544 miles

C 776 miles

D 1,088 miles

12 Ron wrote a check $37.80. Before he wrote the check, his balance was $137.75. What is his new balance?

F $100.15

G $100.00

H $99.95

J $175.55

13 A plant grew $2\frac{3}{4}$ inches in one month, and $3\frac{3}{4}$ inches the next. How many inches did the plant grow in these two months?

A $5\frac{1}{4}$ inches

B $5\frac{1}{2}$ inches

C $6\frac{1}{4}$ inches

D $6\frac{1}{2}$ inches

14 Matt borrowed $800 from his brother. If he pays his brother at the rate of $20 a month, how many months will it take to repay the loan?

F 10

G 20

H 30

J 40

15 Maria put twice the amount of chocolate chips in a cookie recipe. The recipe recommended $1\frac{1}{2}$ cups. How many cups of chips did Maria add?

A 2

B $2\frac{1}{2}$

C 3

D $3\frac{1}{2}$

16 Ella spends $50 a month for her cell phone. How much does she pay for her cell phone in a year?

F $500

G $600

H $1,000

J $1,200

Check your answers on page 125–126.

Lesson 35 Reasonableness of an Answer

You see a carrying case for your cell phone that you would like to buy, but you're not sure if the case is wide enough. The clerk asks for an estimate of the width of your cell phone. Your child says, "One foot!" You and the clerk know that this is not a reasonable estimate.

You will find questions on the TABE that ask you to use your judgment to decide if an answer is reasonable.

Example Which is the best estimate for the width of a cell phone: 1 centimeter, 6 inches, or 2 inches?

Step 1. How wide is 1 centimeter? A centimeter is less than half an inch. In this case, a centimeter is too small.

1 inch = 2.54 centimeters
1 yard = 0.944 meters

Step 2. How wide is 6 inches? The length of your hand is about 6 inches. Now imagine a cell phone and a 6-inch width. Six inches is too large. The width of a cell phone would probably be less than half of this estimate.

A good estimate for the width of a cell phone is 2 inches.

Test Example

Read the question. Circle the answer.

1 If a basketball court is 94 feet long, about how far must a player throw a ball from the centerline to make a basket?

A less than 30 feet

B greater than 30 feet, less than 40 feet

C greater than 40 feet, less than 50 feet

D greater than 50 feet

> **TABE Strategy**
>
> Use what you know about a situation and the size of the number in the problem to decide if an estimate makes sense.

1 **C greater than 40 feet, less than 50 feet** This is a good estimate because shooting from the center to the basket is about 50 feet (the length of the court divided by 2). Option A is not a good estimate because if half of a court is about 50 feet, 30 feet is not enough distance. Option B is also too short. Option D is greater than the distance from centerline to basket.

Read the questions. Circle the answers.

1 If a pizza is about the size of a dinner plate, which of these is the best estimate of the diameter* of the pizza?

A 2 centimeters

B 25 centimeters

C 1 meter

D 10 meters

2 Kara needs a box to pack a plate with a diameter of 6 inches. Which of these is the smallest size box that the plate will fit into?

F 5 in. × 6 in.

G 5 in. × 7 in.

H 7 in. × 7 in.

J 8 in. × 8 in.

3 Andrew has a photo that is 4 in. × 6 in. What is a good estimate of the size frame he should buy for the photo?

A 1 cm × 2 cm

B 12 cm × 20 cm

C 1 meter × 2 meters

D 12 meters × 20 meters

4 Pete wants to plant grass in front of his house. The front yard measures 4 feet by 4 feet, minus a tree that is about 1 foot in diameter. What is a good estimate of the amount of sod it will take to cover this space?

F less than 12 square feet

G greater than 12 square feet, less than 14 square feet

H greater than 14 square feet, but less than 16 square feet

J greater than 18 square feet

5 Sean wants to buy a DVD player. How many months will it take him to save $360, if he saves $30 a month?

A 6 months

B 12 months

C 18 months

D 24 months

6 Alicia travels 26 miles one way to work. How many miles does she travel to work and back in 5 days?

F 31 miles

G 260 miles

H 130 miles

J 520 miles

7 What is the total cost of the following items: a parka for $199.95, boots for $79.95, and a camp chair for $45.00?

A $313.80

B $323.90

C $324.90

D $424.90

8 What is the total amount of liquid if these ingredients are added together: $\frac{1}{3}$ cup honey; $2\frac{1}{3}$ cups water; $\frac{1}{3}$ cup lemon juice?

F 2 cups

G 3 cups

H $3\frac{1}{3}$ cups

J $3\frac{2}{3}$ cups

* Diameter is the distance from one side of a circle to the other through the center.

Check your answers on page 126.

Lesson 36 Rounding

At a flea market, you find an old radio you want to buy. The radio is marked $2.25. You have 2 dollar bills, but you fumble for change. The seller says, "Just give me $2.00." The seller has rounded the price to the nearest whole number. On the TABE you will have to be able to round decimals and whole numbers.

Example If a bride invites 86 people to her wedding and the groom invites 83, what numbers would you use to estimate the total number of people invited?

Step 1. Round 86 to the nearest ten by looking at the digit in the ones place (6). Since the digit in the ones place is greater than 5, round up to 90.

Step 2. Round the number 83 to the nearest ten. Since the digit in the ones place (3) is less than 5, round down to 80.

Add the numbers 90 and 80 to get an estimate.

Example If there are 50 chairs in 9 rows, about how many can be placed in one row?

Round 9 up to 10 because 9 is greater than 5. Now it is easy to calculate. Divide 50 chairs among 10 rows: 50 ÷ 10 = 5.

About 5 chairs can go in each row.

Example Round 73.59 to the nearest whole number.

Step 1. Since you're rounding to a whole number, the answer will be a whole number without decimals.

Step 2. Look at the digit to the right of the decimal point. (73.59) If the digit is 5 or more, round the whole number up to 74. Drop the decimal point and the numbers after it.

73.59 rounded to the nearest whole number is 74.

Test Example

Read the question. Circle the answer.

1   Harry finds 80 tiles at a cost of $44.00. About how much does one tile cost?

  A $0.50   C $1.50

  B $1.00   D $2.00

Hint

Multiply each option by the number of tiles to get a price. Then compare prices to the price in the question.

1   **A $0.50** $44 ÷ 80 = $0.55 Although you could round up to $1.00 (Option B), $0.50 is the best estimate because it is much closer to $0.55 than it is to $1.00. Options C and D are too far away from $0.55 to be reasonable estimates.

Read the questions. Circle the answers.

1 A carton of 12 bottles of water costs $8.64. The cost of each bottle of water is about

A 60 cents.

B 70 cents.

C 65 cents.

D 80 cents.

2 Amy counted the number of cows she saw on a three-day road trip. She counted 32 the first day, 28 the next day, and 46 the third day. If you are estimating by rounding to the nearest ten, what numbers should you use for the number of cows Amy counted on each day?

F 30, 30, and 40

G 30, 40, and 50

H 40, 30, and 50

J 30, 30, and 50

3 To send a package to Mexico via the Fast Freight Company, the charge is $8.40 for the first 10 pounds, plus $2.25 for each extra pound. About how much will it cost to send a 12-pound package?

A $11.00

B $12.00

C $13.00

D $14.00

4 A crate of 120 grapefruit costs $66. At this price, about how much does one grapefruit cost?

F $2.00

G $0.50

H $1.50

J $1.00

5 Which of these decimals when rounded to the nearest whole number is 98?

A 97.45

B 97.61

C 98.72

D 98.51

6 Lisa is having a three-day garage sale. On the first day she had 18 customers, on the second day she had 22 customers, and on the third day she had 34 customers. If you estimate by rounding to the nearest ten, what numbers should you use for the number of customers for each of the days?

F 20, 30, and 30

G 10, 30, and 30

H 20, 20, and 30

J 20, 30, and 40

7 A mail order company charges to send packages to customers. Shipping charges are $5.75 for packages up to ten pounds, and $0.75 for each pound over ten pounds. About how much will it cost to send a 12-pound package?

A $6.00

B $7.00

C $8.00

D $9.00

Check your answers on pages 126–127.

Lesson 37 Estimation

You head for the refreshment stand at the movie theater. You have $7.00. You want a large bag of popcorn, which is $3.75, and a large drink, which is $2.35. You quickly **estimate** that both will cost **about** $6.00. You decide that you have enough money. Estimation is useful when you need to make a quick decision. *Estimate* means to calculate an approximate value for a number, to make the number easier to work with. The TABE will test your ability to estimate numbers involving dollar amounts, measurements, and fractions.

Example At a rummage sale, Tina found a picture frame for $3.70, a sweater for $2.60, and a coffee maker for $5.20. About how much is the total cost?

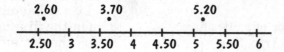

Step 1. Look at the number line above. $3.70 is closer to $4.00 than it is to $3.00. Round $3.70 up to **$4.00**.

Step 2. $2.60 is closer to $3.00 than it is to $2.00. Round $2.60 up to **$3.00**.

Step 3. $5.20 is closer to $5.00 than $6.00. Round $5.20 down to **$5.00**.

Step 4. Add all the numbers you rounded to get an estimate.
$4.00 + $3.00 + $5.00 = $12.00

An estimate of the total cost is $12.00.

Test Example

Read the question. Circle the answer.

1 If a birthday cake is baked in a $12\frac{1}{2} \times 9\frac{1}{4}$ inch pan, about how many 1-inch-square cake servings can be made at a time?

A 20

B 80

C 100

D 120

> **TABE Strategy**
>
> Estimation problems are often two-step problems. You may have to round numbers before you add, subtract, multiply, or divide.

> **1 D 120** This number is closest to the area of the baking pan. Round the fractions to whole numbers, then multiply to find the area of the pan (13 × 9 = 117). Option A adds the measurements of the pan. Options B and C are too small because 13 × 9 is larger than both 80 and 100.

Read the question. Circle the answer.

1 At a used-book sale, Mark bought a history book for $3.25, a cookbook for $2.65, and a paperback book for $1.75. Which number sentence should you use to estimate how much money he spent?

A $3.00 + $2.00 + $1.00 = □

B $3.00 + $3.00 + $1.00 = □

C $4.00 + $2.00 + $2.00 = □

D $3.00 + $3.00 + $2.00 = □

2 Jared spent $37.25 for a movie and dinner. His entertainment budget for the month is $75.00. His night out cost about

F $\frac{1}{3}$ of this amount.

G $\frac{1}{2}$ of this amount.

H $\frac{1}{4}$ of this amount.

J $\frac{3}{4}$ of this amount.

3 Sumi has $32.00 in cash. She stops at a gas station and fills her car with $11.50 worth of gas. The cost of the gas is about

A $\frac{1}{4}$ of her cash

B $\frac{1}{3}$ of her cash

C $\frac{1}{2}$ of her cash

D $\frac{3}{4}$ of her cash

4 Jake is paving a small yard with 1-foot-square paving stones. If the yard is $6\frac{1}{3}$ feet × $8\frac{3}{4}$ feet, about how many 1-foot-square paving stones should he buy?

F 15

G 30

H 50

J 70

5 Selma's monthly food budget is $325.00. She has spent $198.20 so far this month. Selma has spent about

A $\frac{1}{3}$ of her budget

B $\frac{1}{2}$ of her budget

C $\frac{1}{4}$ of her budget

D $\frac{2}{3}$ of her budget

6 Which of these decimals when rounded to the nearest whole number is 32?

F 31.91

G 31.25

H 32.86

J 32.57

7 A basketball court is 94 feet long. In a practice shot, a player makes a basket from halfway to the centerline on the opposite side of the court. About how far did the ball travel?

A greater than 90 feet

B greater than 100 feet

C less than 80 feet

D less than 47 feet

8 Which of these is the best estimate for the width of a bedroom window?

F 1 centimeter

G 5 centimeters

H 1 meter

J 5 meters

Check your answers on page 127.

Read the questions. Circle the answers.

1 Arturo plans to wallpaper a kitchen. He will put paper on a wall that measures 8 feet by 12 feet, but has a 1-foot-square vent. What is a good estimate of the amount of wallpaper he needs for this wall?

A less than 90 square feet

B less than 96 square feet, greater than 90 square feet

C less than 100 square feet, greater than 96 square feet

D more than 100 square feet

2 Attendance for the block-party picnic over the last three years was 23, 46, and 48. If you estimate by rounding to the nearest ten, what numbers should you use for the number of attendees for each year?

F 20, 40, and 40

G 20, 40, and 50

H 30, 40, and 50

J 20, 50, and 50

3 Which of these decimals when rounded to the nearest whole number is 54?

A 54.81

B 52.65

C 53.85

D 53.40

4 Tara is shopping for food for a picnic. Hot dogs cost $3.85, buns cost $1.29, and chips cost $1.59. Which number sentence should you use to estimate how much money she spent?

F $3.00 + $1.00 + $1.00 = ☐

G $4.00 + $2.00 + $2.00 = ☐

H $3.00 + $1.00 + $2.00 = ☐

J $4.00 + $1.00 + $2.00 = ☐

5 You buy a bag of peanuts that weighs 30 ounces. At $1.59 a pound, about how much does the bag of peanuts cost?

A $2.00

B $3.00

C $5.00

D $6.00

6 Which of these is the best estimate for the thickness of a frame around a photograph?

F 1 centimeter

G 25 centimeters

H 1 meter

J 5 meters

7 Rosa bought a dress for $95.50. Her clothing budget for the year is $400. About how much of her budget did she spend?

A $\frac{1}{4}$ of her budget

B $\frac{1}{3}$ of her budget

C $\frac{1}{2}$ of her budget

D $\frac{3}{4}$ of her budget

8 Adam runs 5 miles to the park every day. At the park, he runs on the jogging track for another 3 miles. Then he runs home again. About how many total miles does he run each day?

F 8 miles

G 10 miles

H 15 miles

J 20 miles

9 Gina packed a mirror that is 10 inches wide and 14 inches in height. She packed 1 inch of newspaper around the perimeter to keep it from breaking. What is the smallest size box that she can use?

A 10 × 14 in.

B 11 × 15 in.

C 14 × 18 in.

D 18 × 18 in.

10 Which of these decimals when rounded to the nearest whole number is 49?

F 49.2

G 49.6

H 48.4

J 47.8

11 A box of 12 pens costs $5.99. About how much does one pen cost?

A $0.50

B $0.40

C $1.00

D $1.50

12 Jason's average hits per game for the last three months are: 3.6, 4.5, and 6.2. What are his averages, rounded to the nearest whole number?

F 3, 4, and 6

G 4, 4, and 6

H 4, 5, and 6

J 4, 5, and 7

13 Yoko calculated the monthly cost of caring for her cat: kitty litter $9.99; food $5.85; savings for yearly check-up $5.75. Which number sentence should you use to estimate how much money she spends on her cat every month?

A $9.00 + $6.00 + $5.00 = ☐

B $10.00 + $6.00 + $5.00 = ☐

C $10.00 + $6.00 + $6.00 = ☐

D $10.00 + $6.00 + $7.00 = ☐

14 Anya spent $32 of the $63 she received for her birthday. She spent about

F $\frac{1}{4}$ of the amount

G $\frac{1}{3}$ of the amount

H $\frac{1}{2}$ of the amount

J $\frac{2}{3}$ of the amount

15 If a tennis court is 78 feet long and a player hits the ball from one end of the court into the net, about how far does the ball go?

A greater than 70 feet, less than 80 feet

B greater than 40 feet, less than 50 feet

C less than 10 feet

D less than 50 feet

16 John measured the width of his driveway. Which of these is the best estimate of the width of a driveway?

F 3 centimeters

G 30 centimeters

H 5 meters

J 50 meters

Check your answers on pages 127–128.

Lesson 38 Solve Problems

Sometimes you have to figure out problems that require step-by-step thinking to arrive at a logical conclusion. You have to look at every part of the problem before you arrive at the correct answer. On the TABE, you will be given problems that can be solved by logical reasoning.

Example **What number is inside the square and the triangle, but outside the circle?**

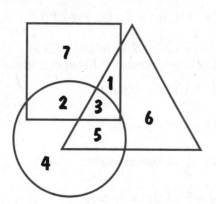

Step 1. Break down the problem into a series of questions. Look at the first thing you have to figure out. What numbers are inside the square? 1, 2, 3, and 7 are inside the square.

Step 2. You have figured out which numbers are inside the square. Which of those 4 numbers are also inside the triangle? Only 1 and 3 are inside the triangle.

Step 3. Decide if 1 or 3 is outside the circle. Look at the diagram. Is 3 outside the circle? No, so 3 is not the answer to the problem. Is 1 outside the circle? Yes.

The 1 is inside the square and the triangle, but it is outside the circle.

Test Example

Read the question. Circle the answer.

1 What number is inside the triangle and the square but outside the circle?

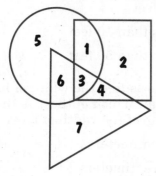

A 1	C 4
B 3	D 6

TABE Strategy

Break down the problem into a series of questions and answer each question to find the solution.

1 **C 4** The 4 is inside the triangle and inside the square, but it is outside the circle. Option A is inside the square and the circle. Option B is inside the triangle, square, and circle. Option D is inside the circle and the triangle.

Practice

Read the questions. Circle the answers.

1 What number is inside the triangle and circle but outside the square?

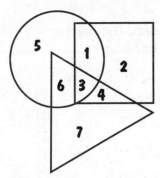

A 1
B 3
C 4
D 6

2 Which of these pictures shows intersecting lines?

  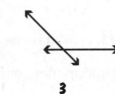

1   2   3

F picture 1 only
G picture 2 only
H pictures 1 and 2 only
J pictures 2 and 3 only

3 What is the name of the following shape?

A cylinder
B cone
C sphere
D circle

4 Which of these numbers is divisible by 2, divisible by 3, and divisible by 7?

F 14
G 21
H 30
J 42

5 Jed had a $5 bill and three $1 bills. If he spends $4.10, how much money does Jed have left?

A $1.90
B $3.10
C $3.90
D $5.30

6 Which of these solid figures is not named correctly?

pyramid   sphere   cone   cube
F   G   H   J

Check your answers on page 128.

Lesson 39 | Missing/Extra Information

Sometimes when you use math in everyday situations, you have exactly the information you need to solve a problem. However, there are times when you may need more information to figure out an answer. In some problems, you may have more information than you need. Then you must decide which information to use.

Example 1 Mark wants to build a fence around his rectangular garden. The garden is 30 feet long. How much fence material does Mark need?

Step 1. List what information you need.
The garden is a rectangle so you need to know its length and its width.

Step 2. List the information that is available.
Length = 30 feet

Step 3. Decide if you need more information, less information, or if you have all the information that you need.
The width of the garden is missing.

Example 2 Lisa left home at 6:00 a.m. and arrived at work at 6:45 a.m. She left work at 4:45 p.m. and arrived home at 5:30 p.m. How long was she at work?

Step 1. List what information you need.
You need to know when Lisa arrived at work and when she left work.

Step 2. List the information that is available.
Left home 6:00; arrived at work 6:45; left work 4:45; arrived home 5:30

Step 3. Decide if you need more information, less information, or if you have the information that you need.
You do not need to know when she left home or arrived at home to solve the problem. You have extra information.

Test Example

Read the question. Circle the answer.

1   The product of 3 numbers is 36. Two of the numbers are 2 and 4. You want to find the third number. You have

   A   extra information.

   B   missing information.

   C   both missing and extra information.

   D   the needed information.

Hint

Always start with a list of information that you need to solve the problem.

1   **D the needed information** You need the product and two of the numbers in order to find the third number. You have exactly the information that you need.

Evaluate each question. Circle the answer that describes the information.

1 Jane jogged for 60 minutes at the track. How far did she jog?

A extra information

B missing information

C both missing and extra information

D the needed information

2 Your bedroom measures 13 feet wide and 14 feet, 6 inches long. It is 7 feet, 9 inches high. You are planning to install a new carpet. How many square feet of carpet will you need?

F extra information

G missing information

H both missing and extra information

J the needed information

3 When Lee looked at the thermometer in the morning, the temperature outdoors was 58°. The temperature dropped 12° between 3:00 p.m. and 7:00 p.m. What was the 7:00 p.m. temperature?

A extra information

B missing information

C both missing and extra information

D the needed information

4 The elevation at the top of a mountain is 12,789 feet. A climbing team has climbed to an elevation of 12,622 feet. How far below the summit are the climbers?

F extra information

G missing information

H both missing and extra information

J the needed information

5 A group of 200 people plan to travel to a political rally. They will get buses that can carry 45 passengers each. How many buses will the group need?

A extra information

B missing information

C both missing and extra information

D the needed information

6 Notebooks cost $3 each, binders cost $4 each, and legal pads cost $1 each. How much will you have to pay if you buy 4 binders, 2 notebooks, and 1 package of pens?

F extra information

G missing information

H both missing and extra information

J the needed information

7 Your brother lives in a city that is 410 miles away. How long will it take for you to travel to his house for a visit?

A extra information

B missing information

C both missing and extra information

D the needed information

8 You are able to type 50 words per minute. A local business pays you $5.00 per page to type documents. If each page of a document has 250 words, how long will it take for you to type a 20 page document?

F extra information

G missing information

H both missing and extra information

J the needed information

Check your answers on page 128.

Lesson 40 Evaluate Solutions

After you solve a problem, it is a good idea to go back and check your answer. You can evaluate the solution by performing the reverse operation. For example, if you multiplied two numbers to reach a solution, you can divide your answer by one of the numbers to check the result.

Sometimes you can evaluate the solution by estimating so you can be certain that your result is reasonable.

Example You need to sew binding around the edges of a square quilt that measures $8\frac{1}{2}$ feet on each side. You calculate that you will need 8 yards of binding for the quilt. Estimate to find out whether your calculation is reasonable.

Step 1. Determine what value you need to estimate.

The binding goes around the perimeter of the quilt. You need to estimate the number of yards in the perimeter.

Step 2. Find the estimated solution.

$8\frac{1}{2}$ feet is about 3 yards. There are 4 sides.
4×3 yards = 12 yards of binding

Step 3. Compare the estimated value to the calculated value.

Your estimate of 12 yards is much larger than the value you calculated. You should repeat your calculation.

Test Example

Read the question. Circle the answer.

1   Check the result of this calculation.
    $14.72 - 8.6 = 5.12$

    A   correct result

    B   result too high

    C   result too low

Hint

When you make an estimate, round the numbers first and then perform the operation.

---

1   C   result too low Because $14 - 8 = 6$ and 0.72 is greater than 0.6, the difference must be greater than 6, so the result was too low.

Applied Math

Evaluate each solution. Circle the answer that describes the result.

1 $76.3 - 44.6 = 41.7$

A correct result

B result too high

C result too low

2 You purchase a table for $148.40, chairs for $106.99, and a lamp for $52.50. The clerk adds the total sale and finds the total cost is $307.89. Use estimation to evaluate the calculation of the total cost.

F correct result

G result too high

H result too low

3 A printer is packing books in boxes for shipment. Each box holds 30 books. He calculates that he will need 50 boxes for a shipment of 1,100 books. Evaluate the solution.

A correct result

B result too high

C result too low

4 When Lisa added $8\frac{2}{3}$ and $6\frac{3}{4}$, she got $14\frac{5}{12}$. Evaluate her solution to the addition problem.

F correct result

G result too high

H result too low

5 A group of 300 people plan to travel to a political rally. They decide they will need 8 buses that can carry 45 passengers each. Evaluate the solution.

A correct result

B result too high

C result too low

6 A farmer delivers eggs to a market in cases that hold 4 dozen eggs per case. He delivers 40 cases and calculates a total of 1,920 eggs. Use estimation to check his calculation.

F correct result

G result too high

H result too low

Check your answers on page 128.

Read these questions. Circle the answers.

Study the diagram. Then do numbers 1 and 2.

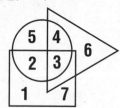

1   What number is in the triangle and the circle but not in the square?

A   2

B   3

C   4

D   5

2   Which number is in the square and the circle but not the triangle?

F   1

G   2

H   3

J   4

3   Two triangles have exactly the same shape but the first triangle is twice as tall as the second triangle. If you want to determine whether the two triangles are congruent, which of the following describes the information you have?

A   extra information

B   missing information

C   both missing and extra information

D   the needed information

4   An elephant in a zoo eats about 200 pounds of food every day. About $\frac{1}{5}$ of that food is fresh vegetables. Keepers need to decide how many pounds of fresh vegetables they need to order each day to feed all of their elephants. Which of the following describes the information you have to solve this problem?

F   extra information

G   missing information

H   both missing and extra information

J   the needed information

5   A traffic engineer counts the vehicles passing an intersection during a four-hour period. The hourly counts were 195, 98, 206, and 480 vehicles. He reported a total count of 1,079 vehicles. Use estimation to evaluate his result.

A   correct result

B   result too high

C   result too low

6   What number would be located halfway between 39 and 83 on a number line?

F   53

G   58

H   61

J   70

7 Which of these numbers is a multiple of 3 and 5, but not a multiple of 4?

   A 20

   B 30

   C 40

   D 60

8 Your car can travel 25 miles for each gallon of gas. The tank holds 15 gallons. Before you leave, you check the price of gasoline and find that it costs $3.19 per gallon. You want to know if a full tank of gas will be enough to take a 225 mile trip without having to stop and refill. Which of the following describes the information you have to solve this problem?

   F extra information

   G missing information

   H both missing and extra information

   J the needed information

9 How many even numbers are there that are less than 31 and divisible by 5?

   A 1

   B 2

   C 3

   D 4

10 It costs 5 cents per page to make copies at a local copy center. You need to make 25 copies of a 48 page report. If you want to find the total cost of making the copies of the report, which of the following describes the information you have to solve this problem?

   F extra information

   G missing information

   H both missing and extra information

   J the needed information

11 Your checking account balance was $1,614. After you wrote checks for $515, $85, and $112, you calculated a balance of $902. Using estimation, find which of the following best describes your result.

   A correct result

   B result too high

   C result too low

12 What point would be located halfway between 19 and 42 on a number line?

   F $30\frac{1}{2}$

   G 28

   H $25\frac{1}{2}$

   J 35

Check your answers on page 129.

The Applied Math Performance Assessment is identical to the real TABE in format and length. It will give you an idea of what the real test is like. Allow yourself 50 minutes to complete this assessment. Check your answers on pages 129–131.

Sample A

What does the 5 in 1,536 mean?

A 5

B 50

C 500

D 5,000

1 Which of these measurements is about the same as 100 inches?

A 40 centimeters

B 250 centimeters

C 5 meters

D 30 meters

2 Which group of numbers is missing from this number pattern?

8, 12, 16, __, __, __, 32

F 17, 18, 19

G 17, 20, 23

H 20, 24, 28

J 22, 26, 30

3 Which of these is the same as the number in the place-value chart?

1,000s	100s	10s	1
1	9	0	4

A 1,994

B 1,000 + 900 + 40

C one thousand nine hundred four

D 1 thousand 9 hundreds 4 tens 0 ones

4 What number is missing from this number pattern?

20, 16, 18, 14, 16, __, 14, 10

F 12

G 15

H 17

J 18

This table shows the cost of daytime phone calls from Chicago to several different cities. Study the table. Then do numbers 5 and 6.

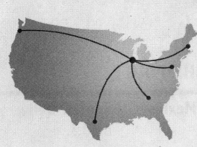

Phone Rates

City	Area Code	First Minute	Each Additional Minute
Cambridge	617	$0.25	$0.22
Atlanta	404	$0.25	$0.22
Washington, D.C.	202	$0.30	$0.32
Portland	207	$0.34	$0.32
San Antonio	210	$0.34	$0.32

5 How much does an 8-minute call to Atlanta cost?

A $1.79

B $2.00

C $1.76

D $2.54

6 A call to San Antonio for 5 minutes costs $1.62. A five-minute call to which other city would be $1.62?

F Atlanta

G Washington, D.C.

H Cambridge

J Portland

Study this table of shipping rates for the Package Express shipping company. Then do numbers 7 through 11.

Package Express

GUARANTEED OVERNIGHT SHIPPING

Weight of Package	Rates within the U.S.	To Mexico	Special Delivery in U.S.
1 oz. to 8 oz.	$1.90	$2.60	$4.60
9 oz to 1 lb.	$3.50	$5.00	$9.00
2 lb.	$6.50	$7.50	$12.50
Over 2 lb.	$1.50 per additional lb.	$2.50 per additional lb.	$3.50 per additional lb.

7 According to the table, how much does it cost to send a 1-pound package to Mexico?

A $2.60

B $3.50

C $4.60

D $5.00

8 According to the table, which of these is the cost of sending a 5-pound package within the U.S.?

F $1.90

G $4.50

H $6.50

J $11.00

9 How much more does it cost to send a 2 pound package by special delivery than to send it with the regular rate within the U.S.?

A $6.00

B $6.50

C $12.50

D $19.00

10 If you want to send a 10-pound package to Mexico, describe the information that you can obtain from the table.

F extra information

G missing information

H both missing and extra information

J the needed information

11 If you want to know the cost per pound to send a 3 pound package to Mexico, what operation would you use?

A $10.00 × 3

B $10.00 ÷ 3

C $10.00 + 3

D $3 ÷ 10.00

12 Solve the equation for n: $8 = n - 2$

   F $n = 6$

   G $n = 10$

   H $n = 12$

   J $n = 16$

13 What temperature does the thermometer show?

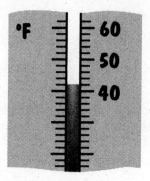

   A 40°F

   B 42°F

   C 44°F

   D 46°F

This table shows the distance from Brighton to four other towns. Study the table. Then do numbers 14 and 15.

Distance from Brighton

Town	Distance (in miles)
Jefferson	36
Springfield	110
Jamestown	165
Dixon	270

14 Anna has driven 40 miles from Brighton toward Dixon. How many more miles does she need to drive before reaching Dixon?

   F 125

   G 230

   H 270

   J 310

15 The drive from Brighton to Jefferson takes about 1 hour. At this driving speed, about how long will it take to get to Jamestown from Brighton?

   A less than 3 hours

   B between 3 and 4 hours

   C between 4 and 5 hours

   D more than 5 hours

This list shows the ingredients needed to make chocolate cookies. Study the list. Then do numbers 16 through 20.

INGREDIENTS

3 cups flour

$1\frac{1}{2}$ cups cocoa powder

$\frac{1}{4}$ teaspoon salt

1 cup plus 6 tablespoons butter

$1\frac{1}{2}$ cups sugar

2 large eggs

2 teaspoons vanilla

16 The amount of sugar needed for the cookies is between

F 1 cup and $1\frac{1}{4}$ cups

G 1 cup and $1\frac{1}{3}$ cups

H $1\frac{1}{4}$ cups and $1\frac{3}{4}$ cups

J $1\frac{3}{4}$ and 2 cups

17 What fraction of an 8-tablespoon stick of butter do you need in addition to 1 cup butter?

A $\frac{1}{4}$

B $\frac{1}{8}$

C $\frac{1}{2}$

D $\frac{3}{4}$

18 When the cocoa powder and the sugar are mixed together, how many cups will the mixture be?

F 2

G $2\frac{1}{2}$

H 3

J $3\frac{1}{2}$

19 If each cookie is a 1-inch square, about how many cookies can be placed side-by-side on a serving tray that measures $8\frac{1}{4} \times 11\frac{3}{4}$ inches?

A 20   C 80

B 60   D 100

20 What fraction of a dozen eggs is used in this recipe?

F $\frac{1}{12}$

G $\frac{1}{4}$

H $\frac{1}{6}$

J $\frac{1}{3}$

TABE Fundamentals: Applied Math

This graph shows average temperatures for a five-week period. Study the graph. Then do numbers 21 through 23.

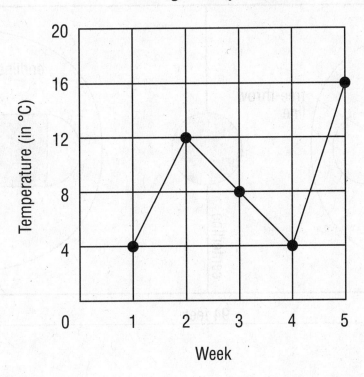

Average Temperature

21 During which two weeks was the average temperature the same?

A Weeks 1 and 2

B Weeks 2 and 3

C Weeks 1 and 4

D Weeks 4 and 5

22 Between which two weeks did the average temperature increase most?

F Weeks 1 and 2

G Weeks 1 and 3

H Weeks 3 and 4

J Weeks 4 and 5

23 The average temperature during Week 6 was 4°C warmer than the average temperature during Week 3. What was the average temperature during Week 6?

A 20°C   C 12°C

B 16°C   D 8°C

This diagram shows the dimensions of a basketball court. Study the diagram. Then do numbers 24 through 26.

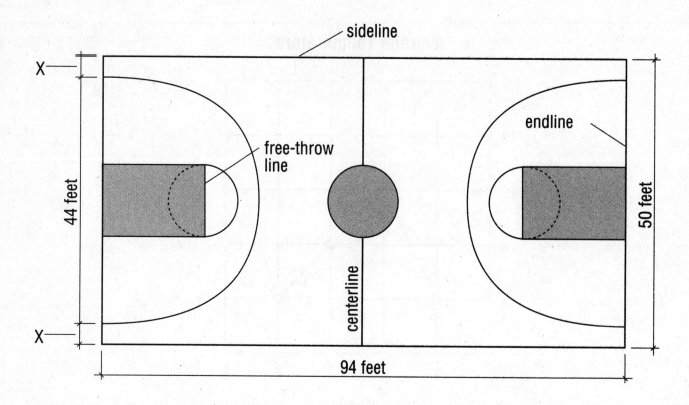

24 What is the length of distance X as shown in the diagram?

   F 3 feet

   G 4 feet

   H 5 feet

   J 6 feet

25 What is the perimeter of the basketball court?

   A 94 feet

   B 138 feet

   C 288 feet

   D 400 feet

26 Which of these lines shows a line of symmetry?

   F centerline

   G sideline

   H free-throw line

   J endline

27 A bottle of juice costs $1.48. About how much will 8 bottles of juice cost?

   A $8

   B $12

   C $16

   D $18

Amy is designing a quilt for her baby nephew. Study this pattern of quilt pieces she will use in her design. Then do numbers 28 through 33.

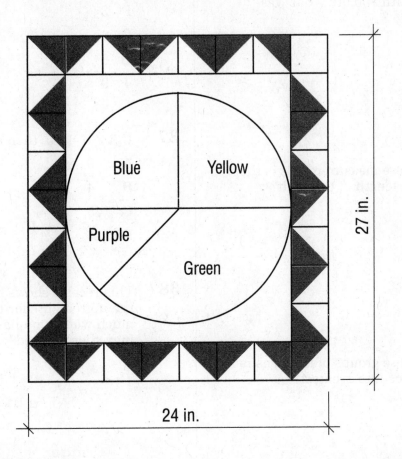

27 in.

24 in.

28 Which of these pieces is missing from the pattern at the upper right-hand corner of the border?

F ◩
H ◪
G ◩
J ◪

29 What pieces of fabric in the circle are congruent?

A the blue and the yellow pieces

B the blue and the purple pieces

C the green and the purple pieces

D the yellow and the green pieces

30 What type of triangle is represented by each of the small gray triangles?

F acute triangle

G equilateral triangle

H obtuse triangle

J right triangle

31 A white cloth border will go around the perimeter of the quilt. How many inches of border will be needed for the quilt?

A 648 inches

B 102 inches

C 108 inches

D 51 inches

32 The materials Amy needed to make the quilt cost $45.72. She paid for the materials with $50.00. What was Amy's change?

F $4.38

G $5.38

H $5.28

J $4.28

33 Which of these measurements is the same as the length of the quilt?

A $2\frac{1}{2}$ feet

B $2\frac{1}{3}$ feet

C $2\frac{1}{4}$ feet

D $2\frac{3}{4}$ feet

34 Which of these groups of fractions is in order from least to greatest?

F $\frac{1}{8}, \frac{1}{3}, \frac{1}{4}$

G $\frac{1}{3}, \frac{1}{2}, \frac{1}{6}$

H $\frac{1}{4}, \frac{1}{3}, \frac{1}{2}$

J $\frac{1}{6}, \frac{1}{2}, \frac{1}{3}$

35 Which of these numbers is a multiple of 8 and a multiple of 6?

A   8

B   36

C   48

D   60

36 Which of these numbers is a common factor of 18 and 24?

F   3

G   4

H   8

J   9

37 If $5 \times n = 45$, then n is

A   9

B   4

C   45

D   225

38 This receipt shows the cost of some of the ingredients for the cookies. How much would you have to pay for the ingredients listed?

```
        Al's Market


    eggs           $1.39
    flour          $1.10
    sugar          $1.29
    vanilla        $2.35
    butter         $2.85
```

F $7.98

G $7.78

H $8.98

J $9.98

Ken has a job installing tile. This picture shows two rows of the tile. Study the picture. Then do numbers 39 through 41.

39 Which of these describes the pattern of tiles in the two rows?

A 1 dark, 1 light

B 1 light, 1 dark

C 2 light, 1 dark

D 2 dark, 1 light

40 Ken left work at 5:15. He arrived at his home at 6:45. How long did it take Ken to get home?

F 1 hour and 15 minutes

G 1 hour and 30 minutes

H 2 hours and 15 minutes

J 2 hours and 45 minutes

41 The box of tiles Ken is using costs $12.90. There are 25 tiles in the box. The cost of each tile is about

A 40 cents

B 50 cents

C 60 cents

D 75 cents

May bought a pair of sunglasses. The check she is writing and her checkbook register are shown below. Study the check and the checkbook. Then do questions 42 through 44.

MAY KIM LEE
535 Argyle Street
Lake Forest, IL 60022

700

Date *March 28, 2004*

Pay to the Order of *Shades, Inc.* $ *12.25*

Twelve and 25/100   Dollars 🔒 Security Features Included. Details on Back.

USPB Federal Savings Bank
707 Bell Street
Lake Forest, IL 60027

Memo *sunglasses*   *May Kim Lee*   MP

⑆ 111987654 ⑆ 1234567890 ⑈ 700

ITEM NO.	DATE	TRANSACTION DESCRIPTION	PAYMENT		√ T	DEPOSIT	BALANCE	
							866.	00
700	3/27	Car Payment	220	00			220	00
							646	00
701	3/28	Shades, Inc.	12	25			12	25

42 What will be the new balance in May's checkbook?

F $634.25

G $633.25

H $634.75

J $633.75

43 If May deposits $45.50, what will her new balance be?

A $679.25

B $588.25

C $633.25

D $45.50

44 May's sunglasses were on sale for $\frac{1}{2}$ of the regular price. Which of these is closest to the regular price?

F $20.00

G $25.00

H $6.00

J $50.00

45 Which number sentence does not have an answer of six when you solve it?

A $5 + 1 = \square$

B $6 - 0 = \square$

C $9 - 4 = \square$

D $4 + 2 = \square$

46 What number goes in the boxes to make both number sentences true?

$17 - \square = 9$

$9 + \square = 17$

F 7

G 8

H 9

J 26

47 Aimee put 25 light bulbs into boxes. Each box holds 4 light bulbs. How many completely full boxes of light bulbs did Aimee have?

A 3   **C** 5

B 4   **D** 6

48 Jack kept track of the number of people who came to the neighborhood block-party meeting for the past three years. He counted 14 people one year, 23 the next, and 27 people for the third year. If you are estimating by rounding to the nearest ten, what numbers should you use to estimate the total number of people Jack counted?

F 10, 20, and 20

G 10, 30, and 30

H 10, 20, and 30

J 20, 30, and 30

49 If the pattern formed by the dots on the blocks continues, how many dots will be needed for the next set of blocks?

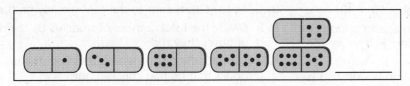

6   15   20   21

A   **B**   **C**   **D**

50 The table shows "Input" numbers that have been changed by a certain rule to get "Output" numbers. Which of these could be the rule?

Input	Output
2	0
3	2
4	4
5	6

F add 3, then subtract 1

G add 4, then subtract 1

H multiply by 2, then subtract 4

J multiply by 2, then subtract 2

Page 117

STOP

Lesson 1 Practice (page 9)

1. **C** The 7 appears in the thousands place. The 7 stands for $7 \times 1,000$ or 7,000.

2. **H** The 1 appears in the thousands place. The 1 stands for $1 \times 1,000$ or 1,000.

3. **D** The 6 appears in the ten thousands place. The 6 stands for $6 \times 10,000$ or 60,000.

4. **G** The 8 appears in the hundreds place. The 8 stands for 8×100 or 800.

5. **A** In option B, the 7 is in the ten thousands place. In option C, the 7 is in the hundreds place. In option D, the 7 is in the ones place.

6. **G** In option F, the 2 is in the hundreds place. In option H, the 2 is in the ten thousands place. In option J, the 2 is in the tens place.

7. **B** In option A, the 5 is in the thousands place. In option C, the 5 is in the tens place. In option D, the 5 is in the hundreds place.

8. **F** The 2 appears in the tens place. $2 \times 10 = 20$.

9. **B** The 4 appears in the tens place. $4 \times 10 = 40$.

10. **H** In option F, 1 is in the thousands place. In option G, it is in the ones place. In option J, it is in the tens place.

11. **D** In option A, 3 is in the ones place. In option B, 3 is in the hundreds place. In option C, 3 is in the thousands place.

Lesson 2 Practice (page 11)

1. **B** There are 5 thousands, 4 tens, and 2 ones.

2. **F** There are three thousands, nine hundreds, and one ten. Since there are no ones, the ones do not have to be mentioned.

3. **D** 0.3210 is the greatest number because the greatest digits are in the places with the greatest value. 0.0123 is the smallest number because the greatest digits are in the places with the least value.

4. **J** 0.7410 is the greatest decimal number because the *greatest digits* are in the places with the greatest value. 0.0147 is the least decimal number because the digits with the *least value* are in the places with the *greatest value.*

Lesson 3 Practice (page 13)

1. **D** Option A equals $16.15. Option B equals $60.50. Option C equals $60.16.

2. **F** Option G equals $40.75. Option H equals $40.42. Option J equals $42.42.

3. **D** Option A equals $70.70. Option B equals $70.00. Option C equals $17.10.

4. **G** Option F equals Twenty and $\frac{65}{100}$; Option H equals Thirty Two and $\frac{65}{100}$; Option J equals Sixty Five and $\frac{23}{100}$

Lesson 4 Practice (page 15)

1. **B** 6 tablespoons of butter is $\frac{6}{8}$ of a stick of butter. Reduce. $\frac{6}{8} \div \frac{2}{2} = \frac{3}{4}$

2. **H** 2 tablespoons is $\frac{2}{16}$ of a bottle of vanilla extract. Reduce. $\frac{2}{16} \div \frac{2}{2} = \frac{1}{8}$

3. **A** Multiply: $\frac{1}{6} \times \frac{6}{1} = \frac{1}{1} = 1$

Lesson 5 Practice (page 17)

1. **A** Add the puppies to the dogs Lisa already has.

2. **G** Add the new cans to the cans already on the shelf.

3. **B** Divide the total number of students by the number of buses they rode.

4. **H** Subtract the books he returned from the number of books that he had checked out.

5. **A** Multiply the number of pencils in a box by the number of boxes in a case.

6. **H** Subtract the day care students from the total students.

7. **D** Multiply the number of tires by the number of cars.

8. **H** Divide the number of pieces by the number of people.

Lesson 6 Practice (page 19)

1. **B** $17 - 8 = 9$ and $9 + 8 = 17$.

2. **F** $13 - 5 = 8$ and $8 + 5 = 13$.

3. **A** The missing number 7 makes both number sentences true: If $12 - 7 = 5$, then $5 + 7 = 12$. Options B, C, and D are incorrect because two different numbers are needed to make the two number sentences in each statement true. For example, option B requires the numbers 3 and 11 to make a "true" statement: If $3 + 4 = 7$, then $11 - 4 = 7$.

4. **G** $9 + 9 = 18$ and $18 - 9 = 9$.

5. **D** The missing number 2 makes both number sentences true: If $6 + 2 = 8$, then $8 - 2 = 6$. Options A, B, and C are incorrect because two different numbers are needed to make the two number sentences in each statement true. For example, option A requires the numbers 8 and 20 to make a true statement: If $14 - 8 = 6$, then $6 + 14 = 20$.

6. F $9 + 5 = 14$ and $14 - 5 = 9$.

7. B When 6 is subtracted from 15, the answer is 9. 6 is also the number to add to 9 for a total of 15.

Lesson 7 Practice (page 21)

1. C 25 cents is an equivalent form of $0.25.

2. F 36 cents is an equivalent form of $0.36.

3. A $7 + 2 = 9$. All the other options are equivalent forms of 8.

4. J $7 - 3 = 4$. All the other options are equivalent forms of 6.

5. B $11 - 2 = 9, 9 + 2 = 11, 11 - 9 = 2$, and $7 - 2 = 5$.

6. G $9 - 3 = 6$

7. A Move the decimal point two places to the right $0.09 = 9$ cents

Lesson 8 Practice (page 23)

1. D $37 \div 6 = 6$, with a remainder of 1. There are 6 full trays, with a remainder of 1 seed.

2. F $40 \div 8 = 5$. Five windows were completely replaced.

3. C $13 \div 5 = 2$, with a remainder of 3. The CD player could be refilled 2 times, with 3 CDs left over.

4. G $26 \div 5 = 5$, with a remainder of 1. Five cars would be completely full, with a remainder of 1 person.

5. C $33 \div 5 = 6$, with a remainder of 3. There would be 6 completely full bags, with a remainder of 3 oranges.

6. G $12 \div 4 = 3$

7. C $20 \div 5 = 4$

8. G $21 \div 7 = 3$

9. D $23 \div 3 = 7 R 2$

Lesson 9 Practice (page 25)

1. A Only A shows all the numbers that evenly divide 9. ($1 \times 9 = 9, 3 \times 3 = 9$)

2. J $1 \times 16 = 16, 2 \times 8 = 16, 4 \times 4 = 16$.

3. D $11 \times 2 = 22$ and $11 \times 8 = 88$.

4. H $8 \times 3 = 24$ and $8 \times 5 = 40$.

5. B $4 \times 5 = 20$ and $4 \times 9 = 36$.

6. G $7 \times 7 = 49$ and $7 \times 8 = 56$.

7. D Carlos can fill 4 cartons of eggs, with 3 eggs left over.

8. F $18 \div 3 = 6; 30 \div 3 = 10$

9. C $15 - 8 = 7$ and $7 + 8 = 15$.

10. H $48 \div 12 = 4; 60 \div 12 = 15$

Lesson 10 Practice (page 27)

1. B All of the points on the number line are 1 apart.

2. J All of the points on the number line are 1 apart.

3. A All of the points on the number line are 2 apart.

4. F All of the points on the number line are 4 apart.

5. A Each of the points on the number line is 2 more than the point to its left. One point to the left of 29 is 27.

6. J There are two segments on the number line between 23 and 25. The difference between these numbers is 2. This tells you that each segment of the number line represents 1. The box is four segments up the number line from 25.

7. B Wednesday is the only day in the chart with a rainfall amount of 6 inches.

8. J Each point on the number line is 1 apart. The box is at 10.

TABE Review Numbers and Number Operations (pages 28–29)

1. C Subtract the number used from the original number. [Operational Sense]

2. F $19 \div 6 = 3$, with a remainder of 1. Luis can fill 3 coolers completely with 1 can left over. [Divisibility]

3. A 18 and 24 both can be evenly divided by 3: $18 \div 3 = 6; 24 \div 3 = 8$. [Factors]

4. G 4 makes both statements true: If $4 + 4 = 8$, then $4 + 4 = 8$. [Properties]

5. D $8 - 4 = 4$. [Equivalent Form]

6. F Each of the points is 1 more. [Number Line]

7. B $7 \times 4 = 28$

8. F $11 - 4 = 7$ and $7 + 4 = 11$. [Properties]

9. C 59 cents is an equivalent form for $0.59. [Equivalent Form]

10. J 72 cents is an equivalent form for $0.72. [Equivalent Form]

11. D $16 - 8 = 8$ and $8 + 8 = 16$. [Properties]

12. G Each of the points is 2 more. [Number Line]

13. B $32 \div 6 = 5$, with a remainder of 2. Marty will completely fill 5 boxes with glasses, with 2 glasses left over. [Divisibility]

14. J $\frac{4}{10} = \frac{2}{5}$ [Fractional Parts]

15. D $3 + 4 = 7$. [Equivalent Form]

Lesson 11 Practice (page 31)

1. D The amount in each of the 4 columns in the row *Insurance* is $122. $122 \times 4 = $488.

2. J The distance from home to the grocery store is 12 miles, and the distance from the grocery store to the school is 12 miles, for a total of 24 miles.

3. C The distance from home to the shopping mall is 12 miles; from the shopping mall to the day care center is 6 miles, and from the day care center to school is 4 miles, for a total of 22 miles. The shortest way back is 18 miles for a total of 40 miles.

4. G The savings is 4 dollars.
$$27 \times 2 = 54$$
$$54 - 50 = 4$$

5. D One 4-line 14-day ad is \$65.85 (\$50.00 + 15.85). The cost of two ads is double \$65.85, or \$131.70.

Lesson 12 Practice (page 33)

1. D If the gas and electric bill doubles, the new amount is \$100 (\$50 × 2). She needs \$50 more since she already has \$50 for the bill. Subtract the amount she needs from her food budget (\$350 − \$50 = \$300).

2. G Kim pays \$465 for rent each month. \$465 × 12 months = \$5,580.

3. C If Kim spends \$120 a month on entertainment, it will take her 4 months to spend \$480 (\$120 × 4 = \$480).

4. J Add all the amounts to find that the total budget is \$1,050. $\frac{465}{1,050}$ is about $\frac{1}{2}$.

5. B $\frac{1}{3}$ of \$120 is \$40 (\$120 ÷ 3 = \$40).

Lesson 13 Practice (page 35)

1. D Only two drivers are needed on Friday.

2. G On Thursday, 5 drivers are needed.

3. C The sum of the car payment and gas is \$250.

4. G The sum of all the expenses is \$1,050.

Lesson 14 Practice (page 37)

1. A A line graph shows change over time.

2. G A bar graph compares different numbers to one another.

3. C A chart is the best display for a list of prices.

4. J The largest segment of the circle graph was the people who drive (45%).

5. B Bar graphs are useful for comparing numbers.

TABE Review: Data Analysis (pages 38–39)

1. B Toast is 90 calories so 3 × 90 = 270 calories. [Graphs]

2. F A candy bar and soft drink would equal 520 calories (220 + 300), the number of calories that Jim wants to substitute. [Graphs]

3. D Both players have an average score of 12 points. [Graphs]

4. H Player 3 scores 4 points a game, and Player 4 scores 20 points a game, for a difference of 16 points. Players 1 and 2 have a difference of 4 points (option F). Players 2 and 3 have a difference of 4 points (option G). Players 1 and 5 have no difference in the number of points scored (option J). [Graphs]

5. A Jay spent a total of \$488.70 for repairs on his car (\$382.70 in February and \$106.00 in April, for a total of \$488.70). To calculate a monthly new car payment, which is $\frac{1}{2}$ of these repair expenses,

divide \$488.70 by 2 to arrive at \$244.35. This is approximately \$250.00. [Tables, Charts, and Diagrams]

6. J If Jay records his monthly expenses, he can add the expenses to see what his car is costing him over a longer period. He may decide it isn't worth keeping an old car if it is costing him too much money. [Tables, Charts, and Diagrams]

7. D The distance from Harrisburg to Oakton is 300 miles; the distance from Oakton to Scottsville is 150 miles; the distance from Scottsville to Bloomington is 325 miles (300 + 150 + 325 = 775). [Tables, Charts, and Diagrams]

8. J The distance Bloomington to Springfield is 270 miles; the distance from Springfield to Scottsville is 250 miles; the distance from Scottsville to Oakton is 150 miles and the distance from Oakton to Harrisburg is 300 miles (270 + 250 + 150 + 300 = 970). [Tables, Charts, and Diagrams]

Lesson 15 Practice (page 41)

1. B There is one choice of Wednesday out of 7 possible choices.

2. G There are 4 Es out of 20 choices. $\frac{4}{20} = \frac{1}{5}$

3. C There are two possibilities and one of them is heads. $\frac{1}{2} = 50\%$

4. F There are four possible choices and 2 are greater than \$8. $\frac{2}{4} = \frac{1}{2}$

5. B There are 5 red marbles of 15 total. $\frac{5}{15} = \frac{1}{3}$

6. H $\frac{1}{2} = 50\%$

7. B There are 17 possible students with red hair of 100 total. $\frac{17}{100} = 17\%$

8. H There is one 5 out of 8 sections.

Lesson 16 Practice (page 43)

1. C 6 + 8 + 10 = 24; 24 ÷ 3 = 8

2. G 4 + 2 + 0 + 4 + 1 + 1 = 12; 12 ÷ 6 = 2

3. B 5 + 3 + 12 + 4 = 24; 24 ÷ 4 = 6

4. G 5 + 1 + 1 + 1 = 8; 8 ÷ 4 = 2

5. C 170 + 150 + 130 + 190 = 640; 640 ÷ 4 = 160

6. G Gloria can fill 7 crates with apples, with 3 leftover.

7. A 12 + 15 + 9 + 12 = 48; 48 ÷ 4 = 12

8. J 12 × 12 = 144

TABE Review: Probability and Statistics (pages 44–45)

1. D 3 + 7 + 8 = 18; 18 ÷ 3 = 6

2. G $\frac{1}{6}$, There is one 3 out of 6 possibilities

3. B 3 + 4 + 8 = 15; 15 ÷ 3 = 5

4. J There is no chance of rolling a 9.

5. A 12 + 12 + 12 + 12 = 48; 48 ÷ 4 = 12

6. J The object is certain to drop.

7. A $30 \div 5 = 6$

8. G There are 4 black kittens out of 12 total

9. B $20 + 25 + 30 = 75$; $75 \div 3 = 25$

10. F Joe has 1 chance in 100 which is 1%

11. C $20 \div 5 = \dfrac{1}{4} = 25\%$

12. H $85 + 90 + 93 + 88 = 356$; $356 \div 4 = 89$

13. B There are six chances out of 120 $\dfrac{6}{120} = \dfrac{1}{20}$

14. G $16 \div 8 = 2$

15. C $\dfrac{5}{26}$, There are 5 vowels of 26 total letters

16. G $22 + 20 + 30 + 14 + 24 = 110$; $110 \div 5 = 22$

Lesson 17 Practice (page 47)

1. D After the first four blocks, the pattern repeats, so a block like the fourth block is the final one that is missing in the pattern. Options A, B, and C do not continue the pattern.

2. F The pair of circles for Option F fit the missing circles in the pattern. Option G would not fit the pattern exactly. Options H and J do not fit any of the pairs of circle patterns.

Lesson 18 Practice (page 49)

1. C 3 is added to each number in the sequence ($24 + 3 = 27$; $27 + 3 = 30$; $30 + 3 = 33$).

2. J The pattern in the number sequence is to add 5, then subtract 1 ($13 + 5 = 18$; $18 - 1 = 17$; $17 + 5 = 22$).

3. C $3 \times 3 = 9$, $9 - 2 = 7$; $2 \times 3 = 6$, $6 - 2 = 4$; $1 \times 3 = 3$, $3 - 2 = 1$.

4. F $180 - 5 = 175$; $175 + 3 = 178$; $178 - 5 = 173$; $173 + 3 + 176$; and so on.

5. C Count the number of dark and light tiles carefully.

Lesson 19 Practice (page 51)

1. D $x + 6 - 6 = 8 - 6 = 2$

2. F $y - 5 + 5 = 4 + 5 = 9$

3. D $6 + 3 = h - 3 + 3 = 9$

4. F $5 - 2 = n + 2 - 2 = 3$

5. B $h \times 2 \div 2 = 14 \div 2 = 7$

6. F $y \div 3 \times 3 = 3 \times 3 = 9$

7. B $m \times 4 \div 4 = 28 \div 4 = 7$

8. J $8 \times 2 = x \div 2 \times 2 = 16$

TABE Review: Patterns, Functions, and Algebra (pages 52–53)

1. B The pattern is add 4, subtract 3. Option A subtracts 3 and then adds four, which does not work in the blanks in the number sequence. Option C begins with adding 2 and therefore does not fit the pattern. Option D adds 1 then adds 3, which does not fit the pattern. [Functions and Patterns]

2. H The pattern in the number sequence is to divide by 5, multiply by 10. Option F does not work because

it adds 10. Option G adds 26. Option J adds 46. [Functions and Patterns]

3. A $1 + 2 = 3$, $3 + 1 = 4$, and so on. Option B would make the second number in the pattern 4 and the third number 6. Option C would make the second number 2 and the third number 5. Option D would make the second number 4 and the third number 8. [Functions and Patterns]

4. G The numbers increase in value by 2. Option F increases by 1. Option H adds 2, then adds 3. Option J includes numbers that increase by 2 but does not follow the 11 in the number sequence. [Functions and Patterns]

5. D

6. G Triangle, circle

7. A $48 \div 6 = 8$. Option B would make the untrue statement $48 \div 40 = 8$. Option C would result in the untrue statement $48 \div 56 = 8$. Option D would result in the untrue statement $48 \div 384 = 8$. [Missing Element]

8. F First find the total number of eggs: $2 \times 12 = 24$. Then divide by the number of eggs in each cake to find the number of cakes: $24 \div 4 = 6$. Option G only multiplies the number of cartons by the number of cakes (2×4). Option H is the sum of all the numbers in the problem ($2 + 12 + 4$). Option J is the product of 2×12, which is only the first step in solving the problem. [Strategy Application]

9. D 70

10. J First find out how many bags of dog food there are in all: 3 bags $\times$ 3 dogs = 9 bags total. Then find out how many bowls there are: 9 bags $\times$ 8 bowls = 72. Option F is the total number of bowls for one dog. Option G is the sum of adding all the numbers in the problem ($3 + 3 + 8$). Option H is the result if you add 3 and 3 and then multiply by 8. [Strategy Application]

11. D $x - 5 + 5 = 6 + 6 = 11$ [Expressions and Equations]

12. H 60

13. A If 3 is substituted for *n*, it results in a true statement (24 × 3 = 72). Option B makes an untrue statement. (24 × 4 ≠ 72). Option C is incorrect because 24 × 48 ≠ 72. Option D is the sum of 24 + 72. [Missing Element]

14. F *y* × 8 ÷ 8 = 48 ÷ 8 = 6 [Expressions and Equations]

Lesson 20 Practice (page 55)

1. D 15 meters is about 45 feet.

2. F 1 centimeter is less than an inch.

3. C One meter is about one yard or 3 feet.

4. G A ceiling is about 8 feet. The other measurements are much smaller or much larger.

5. D One inch measures 2.54 cm so 10 inches is 25.4 cm.

6. H One meter is about 3 inches longer than a yard.

7. D The other measurements are much smaller than a television.

8. F 10 meters is about 30 feet. The other measurements are much too small or too large.

Lesson 21 Practice (page 57)

1. C $3\frac{1}{8}$ inches

2. F 4.4 centimeters

3. B $2\frac{1}{2}$ inches

4. F 4.7 centimeters

Lesson 22 Practice (page 59)

1. C Starting at 10:40, count ten 5-minute (10 × 5 min. = 50) segments, to 11:30.

2. G 9:15 to 11:15 is 2 hours, and 11:15 to 11:30 is 15 minutes.

3. C 7:55 to 8:55 is 1 hour, and 8:55 to 9:15 is 20 minutes.

4. G The shortest route is Alton to Hereford (2:10), Hereford to Kent (1:50), and Kent to Bellville (2:20). 2:10 + 1:50 + 2:20 = 5 hours and 80 minutes = 6 hours and 20 minutes.

5. D The shortest route is Alton to Ash (1:45), Ash to Caldwell (1:50), and Caldwell to Meade (0:50). 1:45 + 1:50 + 0:50 = 2 hours and 145 minutes = 4 hours and 25 minutes.

Lesson 23 Practice (page 61)

1. A The mercury is level with the 20°F mark. Option B would be one line above 20°F. Option C would be halfway between 20 and 30°F. Option D would be four lines above 20°F.

2. J The mercury is four lines above the 70°F mark. Option F would be level with 70°F. Option G would be one line above 70°. Option H would be halfway between 70 and 80°F.

3. B 3:20 to 4:20 is 1 hour, and 4:20 to 5:05 is 45 minutes.

4. J The mercury is four lines above the 90°F mark. Option F would be level with the 90°F mark. Option G would be one line above 90°F. Option H would be halfway between 90 and 100°F.

5. C Option A would indicate that Jack arrived at 11:00. Option B would indicate that Jack arrived at 11:15. Option D would indicate that Jack arrived at 12:10.

6. G The mercury is one line above 0°F. Recall that each line represents a 2°F difference. Option F would be one line lower. Option H would be five lines higher. Option J would be one line higher than 20°F.

Lesson 24 Practice (page 63)

1. B One mile is about 0.6 kilometers.

2. H 4,000 kilometers is about 2,400 miles.

3. C 3 miles = 3 × 5,280 feet = 15,840 feet

4. H 6 miles is slightly less than 32,000 feet.

5. B 100 miles is about 160 kilometers. The other distances are much shorter.

6. G 50 kilometers × 0.6 = 30 miles

7. C 200 miles × 1.6 km = 320 kilometers

8. G 8 kilometers is about 5 miles.

Lesson 25 Practice (page 65)

1. C 24 in. × 2 = 48 inches; 18 × 2 = 36; 36 + 48 = 84. Option A only includes 2 sides of the poster (24 in. + 18 in.). Option B multiplies the measurement of one side by 4 (4 × 18 in.). Option D multiplies the measurement of one side by 4 (4 × 24 in.).

2. H 5 ft. + 5 ft. + 5 ft. + 5 ft. = 20 ft.

TABE Review: Measurement (pages 66–67)

1. B 2 meters is about $6\frac{1}{2}$ feet [Appropriate Units]

2. J 12 feet is equal to 4 yards [Appropriate Units]

3. B 250 centimeters; 100 in. × 2.54 cm/in. = 254 cm [Appropriate Units]

4. G 10:35 to 11:35 is one hour, and 11:35 to 12:15 is 40 minutes. [Time]

5. C If you add 55 minutes to 1:00, it will be 1:55. Then add the cooling time, which will be 2:05. Option A only adds the cooling time. Option B only adds the baking time. Option D is nearly two hours, which is too much time. [Time]

6. G The time between 7:30 and 8:00 is 30 minutes. The time from 8:00 to 8:25 is 25 minutes. 30 + 25 = 55, the number of minutes Libby has to catch the last train. Option F would get her to the station on time, but well before the last train leaves. Option H would get her to the station at 8:55, which is after the last train has left. Option J would get her to the station even later than Option H. [Time]

7. A Count up 2 lines above 20°F to reach 24°F. Option B would be 3 lines higher than 20°F. Option C would be 4 lines higher than 20°F and Option D would be halfway between the fourth line and the line marked 30°F. [Temperature]

8. J Count up four lines by twos to get to 88°F, then move up one degree to 89°F which is midway between 88 and 90°F. Option F is one line above 80°F. Option G is 2 lines above 80°F. [Temperature]

9. B 2.8 centimeters [Use Ruler]

10. J To find the perimeter, add 35 + 35 + 54 + 54 = 178 feet of fencing. [Perimeter]

11. C To find the new perimeter, add 4 feet to the original total: 4 + 178 = 182 feet. [Perimeter]

12. H 26 miles × 1.6 = 41.6 [Length and Distance]

13. C 7 centimeters is about 3 inches [Appropriate Units]

14. H 60 × 1.6 = 96

Lesson 26 Practice (page 69)

1. C Every triangle has three angles.

2. J The top angle is greater than a right angle.

3. C An equilateral triangle has three equal angles and three equal sides.

4. H Both triangles include a right angle.

5. B This is the only choice that has three angles.

6. H This is the only choice that has three angles.

Lesson 27 Practice (page 71)

1. A The solid figure is a cube because it is a 3-dimensional figure that has 6 square sides. Options B, C, and D do not describe the figure.

2. G This shape is a cone because it is a 3-dimensional figure that has a flat, round base and pointed top. Options F, H, and J do not describe the solid figure.

3. C The tissue box shown is shaped like a cube; it has six square sides. The other options describe other 3-dimensional figures.

4. J This figure is a cylinder because it is a 3-dimensional figure that has a flat, round base and top, and curved side. Option F is a cube. Option G is a sphere. Option H is a cone.

5. A The figure in option A is not a circle but a sphere. Options B, C, and D are all labeled correctly.

6. H The figure in option H is a rectangle, which is not a 3-dimensional figure. Options F, G, and J are all 3-dimensional figures.

Lesson 28 Practice (page 73)

1. D The net divides the tennis court into equal halves that are identical. Option A indicates the end line of the court, and does not divide it into symmetrical halves. Option B indicates the length of the court. Option C does not divide the court into halves.

2. H Perimeter is 2 × length (2 × 78 ft. = 156 feet) + 2 × width (2 × 36 ft. = 72 feet); 156 ft. + 72 ft. = 228 feet. Option F adds length and width (78 + 36). Option G multiplies width × 4 (36 ft. × 4 = 144 feet). Option J multiplies length × 4 (78 ft. × 4 = 312).

3. D 1 meter is about 3 feet, so 12 meters is about 36 feet.

4. H Distance to the net is half the length of the court; 78 ft. ÷ 2 = 39 feet. The player walks this distance to the net and back again; 39 ft. + 39 ft. = 78 feet. Option F is the width of the court. Option G is only the distance walked to the net, it does not include the distance back to the base line. Option G is double the length of the whole court.

Lesson 29 Practice (page 75)

1. C This figure is similar to the example because its characteristics are the same. Options A, B, and D all include figures that have different characteristics, so they are not similar.

2. J These figures are similar to figure ABCDE because they have the same characteristics, regardless of their size or the way they are turned. Options F, G, and H do not include both figures that are similar to the example.

3. C These figures are similar to ABCD because their characteristics are the same regardless of how they are turned or their size. Options A, B, and D do not list both figures that are similar to the example.

Lesson 30 Practice (page 77)

1. A These two parts are exactly the same in shape and size and therefore are congruent. Options B, C, and D show two parts that are not exactly the same and are not congruent.

2. H These two parts are exactly the same in size and shape. Options F, G, and J are not the same size and shape, so they are not congruent.

3. B Figures 1 and 2 are the same shape and size. Options A, C, and D do not show the same sizes.

4. G Figures 2 and 3 are congruent because they are the same shape and size. Options F, H, and I do not show congruent figures.

5. D Figures 1 and 3 are the same shape and size, so they are congruent. Options A, B, and C do not show congruent figures.

Lesson 31 Practice (page 79)

1. B Option B shows parallel lines. The other options include at least one of the sets of intersecting lines.

2. G This set of lines is crossing at a right angle. Option F shows parallel lines. Option H shows two sets of parallel lines. Option J shows one set of perpendicular lines (set 2) and one set of parallel lines (set 3).

3. A The letter H has parallel vertical sides because if it were folded on the dotted line, the two sides would match perfectly. Options B, C, and D do not show parallel vertical sides because if they were folded on the dotted lines, the two sides would not match up.

4. H The line up the center of the field creates a line of symmetry because it divides the field into two parts that are exactly the same size and shape. Options F, G, and J do not show lines of symmetry.

5. A The lines do not cross, so they are parallel.

TABE Review: Geometry and Spatial Sense (pages 80–81)

1. C 4×12 inches $= 48$ inches $= 4$ feet [Perimeter]

2. J These parts are congruent because they would line up perfectly if they were placed one on top of the other. Options F, G, and H are not congruent because they would not match up exactly. [Congruency]

3. A Count the hours from 1:00 to 2:00 (one hour), then add the number of minutes (0:50). Option B would be a movie ending at 3:10 p.m., option C would be a movie ending at 3:50 p.m., and option D would be a movie ending at 1:50 p.m.

4. F This figure is divided so that if it were folded along the dotted line, the two sides would match exactly. The two sides of options G, H, and J would not match exactly if folded along the dotted lines. [Symmetry]

5. D Both of these sets show lines that are intersecting because the lines cross each other. Options A, B, and C do not show figures where both lines intersect. [Geometric Elements]

6. J This line creates a line of symmetry because if the triangle is folded along this line the two sides would match up perfectly. Options F, G, and H do not create lines of symmetry. [Symmetry]

7. D This figure is a pyramid, not a cone. Options A, B, and C are labeled correctly. [Solid Figures]

8. J These figures follow the given pattern by repeating the first pair of figures. Options F, G, and H do not follow the pattern. [Solid Figures]

9. A The line drawn through the triangle divides the triangle so that if it were folded along the dotted line the two parts would match perfectly. Options B,

C, and D do not show figures that would match up if folded on the dotted line. [Symmetry]

10. H One kilometer is 1,000 meters which is about 1,000 yards.

11. B The pattern is: circle, square, triangle. Options A, C, and D do not follow this pattern. [Patterns and Shapes]

12. J One yard is exactly 36 inches, so 2 yards is exactly 72 inches.

13. D These figures are similar to the example because their angles and sides are alike. Options A, B, and C do not give choices where both figures are similar to the example. [Similarity]

14. H The perimeter is the total of the sides of a figure: 19 ft. + 9 ft. + 19 ft. + 9 ft. = 56 feet. Option F is 19 ft. − 9 ft. Option G is the sum of just the top and one side of the rectangle (9 ft. + 19 ft.). The number in option J would be the area, 19 ft. × 9 ft., which equals 171 square feet.

Lesson 32 Practice (page 83)

1. D Multiply the distance by the number of trips (40 ft. × 7 = 280 feet). Since she walks there and back, double the distance (280 ft. × 2 = 560 feet). Option A subtracts 14 from 40. Option B adds 14 and 40. Option C multiplies 40 feet by 7, but it does not include the distance Kate walks back to her desk.

2. H Add the distance from home to Springfield and the distance from Springfield to New Lenox (70 mi. + 122 mi. = 192 miles). Since they then have to double back, multiply by 2 (192 mi. × 2 = 384 miles). Option F only includes the distance one way (122 + 70 = 192). Option G only includes the round-trip distance between Springfield and New Lenox (122 mi. × 2 = 244 miles). Option J adds an extra 70 miles.

3. A The balance owed is divided by the monthly payment ($1,350 ÷ $225 = 6). For option B to be correct, the balance owed would be have to be $2,025 ($225 × 9). For option C to be correct, the balance owed would be have to be $2,700 ($225 × 12). For option D to be correct, the balance owed would have to be $5,400 ($225 × 24).

4. G $800 ÷ $40 = 20. For option F, the total saved would be $400 ($40 × 10) For option H the total saved would be $1,200 ($40 × 30). For option J the total saved would be $1,600 ($40 × 40).

5. D 8 + 8 + 9 + 9 = 34

6. H The distance of one side is multiplied by 4 (90 ft. × 4 = 360 feet). Option F is only the distance around 2 sides of the yard. Option G is distance around 3 sides of the yard. Option J is the distance all around the yard plus another 90 feet.

7. C 72 centimeters ÷ 6 = 12 centimeters

Lesson 33 Practice (page 85)

1. C ($2.36 + $1.25 + $1.67 = $5.28). Option A does not regroup a 1 to the whole numbers. Option B does not regroup a 1 to the tenths place. Option D regroups 2 instead of 1 to the whole numbers.

2. F Subtract (101.3 − 98.6 = 2.7). Option G does not regroup from the whole number to subtract the tenths. Option H does not reduce the whole numbers in the tens place before subtracting. Option J does not reduce the whole numbers before subtracting.

3. B The price of one pen is multiplied by 3 ($1.25 × 3 = $3.75). Option A does not regroup a 1 to the tenth place. Option C regroups a 1 to the whole number. Option D regroups a 1 to the whole number, and does not regroup a 1 to the tenths place.

4. G $25.01 is subtracted from the balance of $127.00. Option F does not regroup from the tens place to subtract. Option H does not reduce the tens place by 1 after subtracting. Option J adds $25.01 to the balance of $127.00.

5. A 349.2 − 345.8 = 3.4

6. H This distance to work each way is multiplied by 2 (35 mi. × 2 = 70 miles) and 70 miles is multiplied by the number of days traveled (70 miles × 5 = 350 miles). Option F adds the miles one way and the number of days traveled. Option G only includes the miles one way. Option J multiplies the miles per day by 10 instead of 5.

7. D 2.5 + 2.5 + 2.5 + 2.5 + 2.5 = 12.5

Lesson 34 Practice (page 87)

1. C $2\frac{2}{3} + 1\frac{2}{3} = 3\frac{4}{3}$ or $4\frac{1}{3}$. Option A adds only the whole numbers. Option B does not include the $\frac{1}{3}$ left over after adding $\frac{2}{3}$ and $\frac{2}{3}$. Option D incorrectly adds the fractions.

2. F $\frac{1}{4} + \frac{3}{4} = \frac{4}{4} = 1$. Option G incorrectly adds $\frac{1}{4}$ to the answer. Option H incorrectly includes $\frac{3}{4}$ in the answer. Option J doubles the correct answer.

3. C $1\frac{1}{4} + 1\frac{1}{4} = 2\frac{2}{4}$, and $\frac{2}{4}$ reduced to lowest terms is $\frac{1}{2}$, so the answer is $2\frac{1}{2}$. Option A does not include the fractions. Option B does not add the fractions correctly. Option D is $\frac{1}{2}$ cup too much.

4. J $3\frac{2}{3} + 2\frac{2}{3} = 5\frac{4}{3} = 6\frac{1}{3}$. Option F adds the whole numbers incorrectly. Option G adds the fractions incorrectly. Option H does not include the fraction that is left when $\frac{4}{3}$ is changed to a mixed number.

5. D Option A is too small; a 1 should have been added to the tens place. Option B does not regroup a 2 to the tenths place and a 2 to the ones place. Option C does not regroup a 2 to the tenths place.

6. F Option G does not subtract the tenths correctly. Options H and J do not subtract the tens correctly.

7. D $60 is multiplied by 9 months ($60 × 9 = $540). Option A adds the amount saved and the number of months. Option B is the amount saved for 2 months. Option C is the amount saved for 3 months.

8. B $1,400 divided by $70 comes to 20 monthly payments: $1,400 ÷ $70 = 20. For option A to be correct, the monthly payments would have to be $140. $1,400 ÷ $140 = 10. For option C to be correct, the debt would have to be $2,100: $2,100 ÷ $70 = 30. For option D to be correct, the debt would have to be $2,800 ($2,800 ÷ $70 = 30).

TABE Review: Computation in Context (pages 88–89)

1. B 103 + 127 + 102 = 332. Option A only adds two of the numbers: 103 + 102. Option C adds the hours that Darnell worked and the number of months included in the problem. Option D adds 4 to 103 × 4. [Whole Numbers in Context]

2. F To arrive at the correct answer, a 10 has to be regrouped from the tens place before you can subtract. Option G does not reduce the 4 by 1 before subtracting. Option H does not change the value of the decimals before subtracting. Option J does not reduce the 4 by 1 or change the value of the decimals before subtracting. [Decimals in Context]

3. B $60 × 9 = $540. Option A is $60 × 6 = $360. Option C is $60 × 12 = $720. Option D is $1,080. [Whole Numbers in Context]

4. H $1\frac{1}{4} + 1\frac{1}{4} = 2\frac{2}{4}$; $\frac{2}{4}$ reduced to lowest terms is $\frac{1}{2}$, so the answer is $2\frac{1}{2}$. Option F does not include the fraction. Option G does not double $\frac{1}{4}$. Option J is $\frac{1}{2}$ cup too much. [Fractions in Context]

5. C $1\frac{1}{4} + 1\frac{3}{4} = 2\frac{4}{4}$; $\frac{4}{4}$ equals 1 whole, which is added to 2 for an answer of 3 whole cups. Option A does not include the fractions. Options B and D do not add the fractions correctly. [Fractions in Context]

6. J If a player runs back and forth twice, she makes 4 trips: 4 × 94 ft. = 376 feet. Option F is the distance of only one trip. Option G is only trips (2 × 94). Option H is three trips. [Whole Numbers in Context]

7. A 180 bulbs divided by 4 sides equals 45 bulbs per side. Option B divides the number of bulbs by 2 sides. Option C subtracts the number of sides from the number of bulbs. Option D multiplies the number of bulbs by the number of sides. [Whole Numbers in Context]

8. H Option F does not regroup the amount from the hundredths to the tenths. Option G does not regroup the amount from the tenths to the ones. Option J adds 3 to the tens instead of 2. [Fractions in Context]

9. C $4\frac{2}{3} + 2\frac{2}{3} = 6\frac{4}{3}$; $\frac{4}{3} = 1\frac{1}{3}$; $6 + 1\frac{1}{3} = 7\frac{1}{3}$. Option A does not add the fractions correctly. Option B does not include the fraction. Option D adds the whole numbers incorrectly. [Fractions in Context]

10. J $75 \times 16 = \$1,200$. Option F adds 12 months to $75 instead of multiplying. Option G is the amount saved for 6 months. Option H is the amount saved for 12 months. [Decimals in Context]

11. D The miles one way are added and then multiplied by two: 232 mi. + 312 mi. = 544 miles; 544 mi. × 2 = 1088 miles. Option A subtracts the miles driven from one place to the next. Option B only adds the miles one way. Option C adds the miles one way and only half of the miles the other way. [Whole Numbers in Context]

12. H One ten was regrouped to correctly subtract the ones, tenths, and hundredths. Option F does not regroup a ten before subtracting. Option G does not subtract the decimal. Option J adds the amount of the check to the balance instead of subtracting it. [Decimals in Context]

13. D $2\frac{3}{4} + 3\frac{3}{4} = 5\frac{6}{4}$. $\frac{6}{4} = 1\frac{2}{4}$; $\frac{2}{4}$ reduced to lowest terms is $\frac{1}{2}$, so the total of the whole numbers and the fraction is $6\frac{1}{2}$. Option A only adds the whole numbers. Option B does not regroup the whole number when $\frac{3}{4}$ and $\frac{3}{4}$ are added. Option C incorrectly adds the fractions. [Fractions in Context]

14. J $800 ÷ \$20 = 40$. For option F to be true, the amount paid each month would have to be $80 ($800 ÷ $80 = 10$). For option G to be true, the amount paid each month would have to be $40 ($800 ÷ $40 = 20$). For option H to be true, the amount borrowed would have to be $600 ($600 ÷ 20 = 30$). [Whole Numbers in Context]

15. C $1\frac{1}{2} + 1\frac{1}{2} = 2\frac{2}{2} = 2 + 1 = 3$. Option A does not include the fractions. Option B only includes one of the fractions. Option D incorrectly adds the whole numbers and fractions. [Fractions]

16. G The amount per month is multiplied by 12, the number of months in a year ($50 × 12 = 600). Option F is the amount for 10 months ($50 × 10 = 500). Option G is the amount for 20 months

($50 × 20 = \$1,000$). Option J is the amount for 24 months ($50 × 24 = \$1,200$) [Whole Numbers in Context]

1. B This is a reasonable estimate because a centimeter is about $\frac{1}{2}$ inch, so 25 centimeters is about 12 inches, the likely size of a dinner plate. Option A is much too small; 2 centimeters is about an inch. Options C and D are too great of an estimate, because a meter is about a yard.

2. H If the plate has a diameter of 6 inches, the length and width of the box has to be slightly larger to accommodate it. Option F is too small on all sides. Option G is too small on one side. Option J would fit the plate, but it is not the smallest size box that would work.

3. B This is slightly larger than the 4 in. × 6 in. photo. Option A is too small, because 1 cm. is less than 1 inch. Options C and D are not reasonable estimates because a meter is too long.

4. H The area of the yard is 16 square feet, minus the space for the tree, which reduces the square footage by one square foot. Option F is not reasonable because 12 square feet is less than the nearly 16 square feet that is needed. Option G is still too small of an estimate, because the tree only takes up about one square foot. Option J is too large because it would be greater than the whole area, even including the tree.

5. B $360 ÷ \$30 = 12$. For option A to be true, the total amount would have to be $180. For option C to be true, the total amount would have to be $540. For option D to be true, the total amount would have to be $720.

6. G The round-trip mileage per day is 26 mi. × 2 = 52 miles; 52 miles multiplied by 5 days equals 260 miles. Option F only adds the mileage one way plus the number of days. Option H does not include the round-trip mileage per day. Option J doubles the amount of the total mileage.

7. C This is the correct sum for $199.95 + $79.95 + $45.00. Option A does not regroup a 1 to the tenths when adding. Option B does not regroup a 1 to the ones place when adding. Option D incorrectly adds the numbers in the hundreds place.

8. G $\frac{1}{3} + 2\frac{1}{3} + \frac{1}{3} = 2\frac{3}{3} = 3$. Option A does not add the fractions. Option H incorrectly adds another $\frac{1}{3}$. Option J incorrectly adds another $\frac{2}{3}$.

1. B $8.64 ÷ 12 = \$0.72$. $0.72 is rounded down because the 2 in the hundredths place is less than 5. Options A and C are too low. Option D is too great.

2. J 32 is rounded down because 2 is less than 5, 28 is rounded up because 8 is greater than 5, and 46 is rounded up because 6 is greater than 5.

3. C The cost of sending a 10-pound package is $8.40. Add $4.50 for the 2 extra pounds ($2.25 + $2.25) for a total of $12.90. To round $12.90, round up to get $13. Options A and B are too low. Option D is too high.

4. G The cost of the crate of grapefruit is divided by the number of grapefruit to find the price of a single grapefruit: $66 ÷ 120 = $0.55. $0.55 is closest to the number $0.50 than to of any of the other options. The other options are all much too high.

5. B The digit 6 is at least 5, so round up to the next whole number, 98. Option A rounds down to 97. Options C and D round up to 99.

6. H 18 is rounded up to 20 because 8 is greater than 5, 22 is rounded down to 20 because 2 is less than 5, and 34 is rounded down to 30 because 4 is less than 5.

7. B The cost of shipping a ten-pound package ($5.75) is added to the additional charge for the 2 extra pounds. ($0.75 × 2 = $1.50 and $5.75 + $1.50 = $7.25). $7.25 rounded to the nearest whole number is $7.00. Option A is too low. Options C and D are too high.

Lesson 37 Practice (page 95)

1. D $3.25 rounded to the nearest dollar is $3.00, $2.65 rounded to the nearest dollar is $3.00, and $1.75 rounded to the nearest dollar is $2.00. Option A rounds down $2.65 and $1.75 instead of up. Option B rounds down $1.75 instead of up. Option C rounds up $3.25 instead of down, and rounds down $2.65 instead of up.

2. G $37.25 can be rounded up to $40. $75.00 can be rounded up to $80. These dollar amounts are converted to a fraction $\frac{40}{80}$, which reduced to lowest terms is $\frac{1}{2}$. Options F and H are less than $\frac{1}{2}$. Option J is greater than $\frac{1}{2}$.

3. B The numbers $11.50 and $32.00 are rounded down to the nearest ten to become 10 and 30. The numbers are then written as the fraction $\frac{10}{30}$, which reduced to lowest terms is $\frac{1}{3}$.

4. H The fractions $6\frac{1}{3}$ and $8\frac{3}{4}$ are rounded to the nearest whole numbers 6 and 9, then 6 and 9 are multiplied to find the number of square feet in the yard (6 ft. × 9 ft. = 54 square feet). 50 is the closest estimate to this product. Option F adds the length and width of the yard. Option G is only $\frac{1}{2}$ of the number of a stones needed. Option J is too great.

5. D $325.00 and $198.20 are rounded to the nearest hundred, $300 and $200, and converted to the fraction $\frac{200}{300}$, which is then reduced to its lowest terms, $\frac{2}{3}$. Options A, B, and C are all less than $\frac{2}{3}$, and therefore these estimates are too low.

6. F 31.91 rounds up to 32. Option G rounds down to 31. Options H and J round up to 33.

7. C A basketball court is 94 feet long, so the distance from the center to one end is 47 feet (94 ft. ÷ 2 = 47 feet). If the distance to the centerline from a basket is 47 feet, the half of the distance from the centerline to the opposite side is about 24 feet: 47 + 24 is about 80 feet. Options A and B are both too great if the ball will travel only about 80 feet. Option D is only the length of the centerline, which is too low of an estimate.

8. H A meter is about a yard (3 feet), so this is the best estimate. Options F and G are too low. Option J is too high.

TABE Review: Estimation (pages 96–97)

1. B The wall is 96 square feet (8 ft. × 12 ft. = 96 square feet) minus 1 square foot for the vent: 96 square ft. − 1 square ft. = 95 square feet. So, between 90 and 96 square feet is a reasonable estimate. Options C and D are both more than is needed, even including the vent. Option A is too low of an estimate. [Reasonableness of Answer]

2. J 23 is rounded down to 20 because there are fewer than 5 ones, 46 and 48 are rounded up to 50 because both numbers have digits that are at least 5 in the ones place. Option F rounds 46 and 48 down instead of up. Option G rounds incorrectly. Option H incorrectly rounds 23 up and 46 down. [Rounding]

3. C The decimal rounds up to 54. The decimals in option A round up to 55. Option B rounds up to 53. Option D rounds down to 53. [Rounding]

4. J $3.85 and $1.59 round up, and $1.29 rounds down. Option F rounds down all the numbers. Option G rounds up all the numbers. Option H rounds down $3.85 instead of rounding up. [Estimation]

5. B There are 16 ounces in one pound, so 30 ounces is nearly 2 pounds. $1.59 can be rounded to $1.60, so 2 × $1.60 = $3.20. $3.20 can be rounded down to $3.00. Option A rounds the price of only 1 pound. Option C is about the price of 3 pounds. Option D is double the correct estimated amount. [Rounding]

6. F A centimeter is less than $\frac{1}{2}$ inch, so a centimeter is a good estimate. Option G is too wide. Options H and J are both much too large. [Reasonableness of Answer]

7. A $95.50 rounds up to $100. That amount, along with her clothing budget amount, $400, is converted to the fraction $\frac{100}{400}$, which reduced to lowest terms is $\frac{1}{4}$. For option B to be true, Rosa would have to spend about $130 ($400 ÷ 3). For option C to be true, Rosa would have to spend about $200 ($400 ÷ 2). For option D to be true, Rosa would have to spend about $300 ($\frac{300}{400}$, which equals $\frac{3}{4}$). [Estimation]

8. H 5 miles to the park plus 3 miles in the park equal 8 miles. The run home is another 5 miles (5 + 3 + 5 = 13). 13 rounds to 15. Option F is the sum of the miles to the park one way plus the miles on the track. Option G rounds down 13 miles. Option J incorrectly rounds up 13. [Reasonableness of Answer]

9. C 1 inch of packing is added all around the mirror to increase the measurement from 10 in. × 14 in. to 12 in. × 16 in (1 inch for each side—top, bottom, left, and right). Options B and C are smaller than these measurements. Option D would work, but is not the smallest-sized box that works. [Reasonableness of Answer]

10. F Round down to 49. Option G rounds up to 50. Option H rounds down to 48. Option J rounds up to 48. [Rounding]

11. A Round $5.99 up to $6.00. $6.00 divided by 12 is $0.50. Option B is too low. Options C and D are too high. [Rounding]

12. H 3.6 rounds up to 4, 4.5 rounds up to 5, and 6.2 rounds down to 6. Option F incorrectly rounds down all the numbers. Option G incorrectly rounds down 4.5. Option H incorrectly rounds up 6.2. [Rounding]

13. C All of the numbers are rounded up to the nearest whole number. Option A incorrectly rounds down both $9.99 and $5.75. Option B incorrectly rounds down $5.75. Option D incorrectly rounds up $5.75 to $7 instead of $6. [Rounding]

14. H $32 and $63 are rounded down to $30 and $60. Convert the numbers into the fraction $\frac{30}{60}$. This fraction reduced to lowest terms is $\frac{1}{2}$. For option F to be true, Anya would have to spend only $15 ($\frac{15}{60} = \frac{1}{4}$). For option G to be true, Anya would have to spend about $20 ($\frac{20}{60} = \frac{1}{3}$). For option H to be true, Anya would have to spend about $40 ($\frac{40}{60} = \frac{2}{3}$). [Estimation]

15. D Round 78 feet to 80. The net is halfway at about 40 feet, so less than 50 feet is a reasonable estimate. Option A and B are too high because the ball only goes half of the length of the court. Option C is not reasonable because it is only about $\frac{1}{4}$ the length of half a tennis court. [Reasonableness of Answer]

16. H A meter is about a yard, so this is a reasonable estimate, giving about 15 feet. Options F and G are not reasonable because a centimeter is smaller than an inch. Option J is too great an estimate. [Reasonableness of Answer]

Lesson 38 Practice (page 99)

1. D The 6 is the only number that is outside the square and inside both the circle and the triangle. Option A is inside the square and the circle. Option B is inside the square, the circle, and the triangle. Option C is inside the square and the triangle.

2. J Both pictures 2 and 3 show lines that intersect. Option F shows parallel lines. Option G lists only one set of intersecting lines. Option H lists one set of parallel lines and one set of intersecting lines.

3. C This shape is a circular, 3-dimensional figure. Options A, B, and D describe other 3-dimensional figures.

4. J 42 ÷ 2 = 21; 42 ÷ 3 = 14; 42 ÷ 7 = 6

5. C $5 + $1 + $1 + $1 = $8.00; $8.00 − $4.10 = $3.90

6. G This solid figure should be labeled a cylinder. The solid figures for options F, H, and J are all correctly labeled.

Lesson 39 Practice (page 101)

1. B You need to also know how fast she jogged.

2. F You do not need to know the height of the room.

3. B You need to know the temperature at 3:00.

4. J You have the information you need for the calculation.

5. D You have the information you need for the calculation.

6. H You need the price of pens but not the price of legal pads.

7. B You need to know how fast you can travel.

8. F You do not need to know the rate of pay.

Lesson 40 Practice (page 103)

1. B Estimate 75 − 45 = 30

2. F Estimate 150 + 100 + 50 = 300

3. B Estimate 1200 ÷ 30 = 40

4. H 8 + 6 = 14 and the fractions add up to more than 1

5. B 300 ÷ 50 = 6 buses

6. F Estimate 2,000 ÷ 50 = 40

1. C The circle and triangle overlap at number 4 without touching the square. Option A is in the circle and square but not in the triangle. Option B is in all three shapes. Option D is in the circle only.

2. G The circle and square overlap at number 2 without touching the triangle. Option F is only in the square. Option H is in all three shapes. Option J is in the circle and the triangle but not in the square.

3. D You have enough information to know the triangles are not congruent.

4. G You do not know the number of elephants.

5. C Estimate $200 + 100 + 200 + 500 = 1,000$

6. H The difference $83 - 39 = 44$. If you add half that amount to 39, $39 + 22 = 61$.

7. B 30 is a multiple of 3 and 5, but not of 4; 20 is a multiple of 4 and 5 but not 3; 40 is a multiple of 4 and 5 but not 3; 60 is a multiple of 3, 4, and 5.

8. F You do not need to know the price of gasoline.

9. C The only even numbers divisible by 5 are multiples of 10: 10, 20, 30.

10. J You have all the information you need to calculate the cost.

11. A Estimate $1,600 - 500 - 100 - 100 = 900$

12. F The difference is $42 - 19 = 23$. If you add half that amount to 19, $19 + 11\frac{1}{2} = 30\frac{1}{2}$.

Performance Assessment: Applied Math (pages 106–117)

A. C The 5 appears in the hundreds place. The 5 stands for 5×100, or 500. Option A shows the 5 in the ones place, option B, in the tens place, and option D, in the thousands place.

1. B 250 centimeters 100 in $\times$ 2.54 cm/in = 254 cm [Appropriate Units]

2. H The pattern in this number sequence is $+ 4$ ($16 + 4 = 20$, $20 + 4 = 24$, $24 + 4 = 28$). Option F increases numbers by 1, which works with 16, but does not fit the pattern of $+ 4$ between the other numbers in the sequence. Option G adds by 3, and option J adds by 4, so do not match the pattern between any of the numbers in the sequence. [Functions and Patterns]

3. C The numbers are written out to follow the place value from greatest to least value. Option A incorrectly places 9 in the tens place. Option B includes 4 tens (40) instead of 4 ones. Option D also includes 4 tens instead of 4 ones. [Recognize Numbers]

4. F The number pattern in this sequence is $- 4, + 2$. $16 - 4 = 12$, the next number in the sequence; the number that follows 12, is $12 + 2 = 14$. Option G subtracts 1 from 16. Option H adds 1. Option J adds 2. [Functions and Patterns]

5. A $0.25 for the first minute plus $1.54 for the additional minutes ($0.22 $\times$ 7) equals $1.79. Option B would be an 8-minute call at the First-Minute rate ($0.25 $\times$ 8). Option C would be an 8-minute call at the Additional Minute Rate ($0.22 $\times$ 8). Option D calculates using the rate for a call to Washington, D.C. [Tables, Charts, and Diagrams]

6. J The first minutes for a call to Portland is $0.34 plus 4 additional minutes at $0.32 a minute ($0.32 $\times$ 4 = $1.28; $1.28 + $0.34 = $1.62). Options F and H would be $1.13 ($0.25 + $0.88 for the additional 4 minutes). Option G would be $1.58 ($0.30 + $1.28 for the additional 4 minutes). [Tables, Charts, and Diagrams]

7. D Option A is the rate for a package weighing up to 8 oz. Option B is the rate within the U.S. Option C is the Special Delivery rate for up to 8 oz. [Tables, Charts, and Diagrams]

8. J The cost of a 2-lb package is $6.50 plus an additional charge of $1.50 for each of the additional 3 pounds: $6.50 + ($1.50 $\times$ 3 = $4.50) = $11.00. Option F is the rate for the lightest package. Option G is only the additional charge. Option H is the rate for a 2-lb package. [Tables, Charts, and Diagrams]

9. A $12.50 - $6.50 = $6.00 [Tables, Charts, and Diagrams]

10. F You have the information you need to calculate the cost but you also have shipping information for the U. S. [Tables, Charts, and Diagrams]

11. B The cost is $7.50 + $2.50 = $10.00. The cost per pound is $10.00 $\div$ 3 [Tables, Charts, and Diagrams]

12. G $8 + 2 = n - 2 + 2$; $10 = n$ [Expressions and Equations]

13. B The red mark is one line above the 40-degree mark on the thermometer. Each line indicates 2 degrees, so $40°F + 2°F = 42°F$. [Temperature]

14. G The distance from Brighton to Dixon is 270 miles minus the 40 miles already driven ($270 - 40 = 230$). Option F is the distance from Brighton to Jamestown minus what she's already driven. Option H is the distance from Brighton to Dixon. Option J is the distance from Brighton to Dixon plus 40 miles. [Tables, Charts, and Diagrams]

15. C If it takes 1 hour to go about 40 miles (36 rounded up), it will take about 4 hours to go about 4 times as far (round 165 to the compatible number of 160, then divide by 4). Since you rounded down, you know it will actually be a little longer. Options A and B are too low. Option D is too high. [Tables, Charts, and Diagrams]

16. H $\frac{1}{4}$ is a smaller fraction than $\frac{1}{2}$ and $\frac{3}{4}$ is a larger fraction than $\frac{1}{2}$, so $1\frac{1}{2}$ is between $1\frac{1}{4}$ and $1\frac{3}{4}$. Options F and G include amounts that are both smaller than $1\frac{1}{2}$ cups. Option J includes amounts that are both larger than $1\frac{1}{2}$ cups.

17. D You need $\frac{6}{8}$ of a stick of butter; $\frac{6}{8}$ reduced to lowest terms is $\frac{3}{4}$. Option A would be correct if

2 tablespoons were used ($\frac{2}{8} = \frac{1}{4}$). Option B would be correct if 1 tablespoon were used ($\frac{1}{8}$). Option C would be correct is 4 tablespoons were used ($\frac{4}{8} = \frac{1}{2}$). [Fractional Parts]

18. H The whole numbers of each ingredient are added together to equal 2 cups, and the fractions for each ingredient $\frac{1}{2}$ and $\frac{1}{2}$ equal 1. So $1\frac{1}{2} + 1\frac{1}{2} = 2 + 1 = 3$. Option F does not add the fractions. Option G does not add the fraction of one of the ingredients. Option J adds an additional $\frac{1}{2}$ to the total. [Fractions in Context]

19. D The measurements of the tray are rounded to the nearest whole numbers 8 and 12. The area of the tray is 96 square inches (8 in. × 12 in. = 96 square inches), so about 100 cookies will fit on the tray. Options A, B, and C are estimates that are too small based on the area of the tray. [Estimation]

20. H Option F is correct for 1 egg. Option G reduces the fraction incorrectly. Option J is the fractional part of 4 eggs. [Fractional Parts]

21. C The average temperature was 4°C in both Week 1 and 4. Option A includes temperatures that are not the same: 4°C for Week 1 and 12°C for Week 2. Option B's temperatures are 12°C for Week 2 and 8°C for Week 3. Option D's temperatures are 4°C for Week 4 and 16°C for Week 5. [Tables, Charts, and Diagrams]

22. J The temperature increased from 4 to 16 degrees from Week 4 to Week 5, the greatest increase. In option F the temperature increased from 4 to 12 degrees. In option G, it increased from 4 to 8. In option H, the temperature decreased from 8 to 4. [Table, Chart, and Diagram]

23. C Week 3's average temperature was 8°C, 4 is added to that temperature to arrive at 12°C. Option A is 4°C added to Week 5. Option B is 4°C added to Week 2. Option D is 4°C added to Week 1 or Week 4. [Tables, Charts, and Diagrams]

24. F If the portion of the endline labeled is 44 feet, and the entire endline at the other side of the court is labeled 50 feet, then the distance at each end is 3 feet. 2 × 3 = 6; 6 + 44 = 50. Options G, H, and J cannot be doubled and added to 44 to equal 50 feet. [Whole Numbers in Context]

25. C 94 + 94 + 50 + 50 = 288 feet

26. F If the diagram could be folded on the centerline, both sides of the court would make identical halves. Options G and J do not divide the court in half. Option H does not divide the court so that everything is equal on both sides of the court. [Symmetry]

27. B $1.48 is about $1.50; 8 × $1.50 = $12.00 [Estimation]

28. H The other options would not continue the pattern correctly. [Patterns and Shapes]

29. A These pieces are congruent because if one is placed on top of the other, they match. Options B, C, and D do not pair two pieces that match. [Congruency]

30. J Each of the small triangles has one right angle.

31. B Perimeter is the sum of all sides (27 + 27 + 24 + 24 = 102). Option A is the area of the quilt (length × width = 24 inches × 27 inches). Option C is length × 4. Option D is length + width. [Perimeter]

32. J To subtract $45.72 from $50.00, 2 hundredths is subtracted from 10 hundredths, 7 tenths is subtracted from 9 tenths, and 5 is subtracted from 9 ones. Option F does not subtract the tenths correctly. Option G does not subtract the tenths or the ones correctly. Option H does not subtract the ones correctly. [Decimals in Context]

33. C The quilt is 27 inches long. 24 inches is 2 feet and 3 inches is $\frac{3}{12} = \frac{1}{4}$ foot.

34. H The smaller the number of parts that a whole is divided into, the greater the fraction. Option F should be $\frac{1}{8}, \frac{1}{4}, \frac{1}{3}$. Option G should be $\frac{1}{6}, \frac{1}{3}, \frac{1}{2}$. Option J should be $\frac{1}{6}, \frac{1}{3}, \frac{1}{2}$. [Ordering]

35. C 48 is a multiple of both 8 and 6. 36 and 60 are multiples of 6 but not 8. 8 is a multiple of 8 but not 6.

36. F 3 can be multiplied with another number to arrive at both 18 and 24 (3 × 6 = 18; 3 × 8 = 24). Options G and H cannot be multiplied with another number for a product of 18. Option J cannot be multiplied with another number for a product of 24. [Factors]

37. A 5 × 9 = 45 is a true statement. Option B would give 5 × 4 = 45, which is not a true statement. Option C would be 5 × 45 = 45, which is not true. Option D would be 5 × 225 = 45, which is also not a true statement. [Missing Element]

38. H When the prices are totaled, 2 tens are carried to the tenths place and a whole number is added to the ones place. In option F, a 1 was not carried to the ones place. In option G, a 2 was not carried to the tenths place and a 1 was not carried to the ones place. In option J, a 2 instead of a 1 was carried to the ones place. [Decimals in Context]

39. D The pattern is + 2 dark + 1 light. Options A and B indicate an alternating pattern with equal numbers of light and dark tiles. Option C reverses the pattern of color in the tiles. [Functions and Patterns]

40. G From 5:15 to 6:15 is 1 hour. Ken took an additional 30 minutes to travel home, so the total is 1 hour and 30 minutes. Option F is 15 minutes too short. Option H is 45 minutes too long. Option J is 1 hour and 15 minutes too long. [Time]

41. **B** $12.90 can be rounded to the nearest whole number, $13. $13.00 ÷ 25 = $0.52. $0.52 can be rounded down to $0.50, or fifty cents. Option A is a number that is too small. Options C and D are numbers that are too large. [Rounding]

42. **J** To subtract the tenths and hundredths, a 1 from the ones place had to be borrowed. Option F does not subtract the tenths or ones correctly. Option G incorrectly subtracts the tenths. Option H incorrectly subtracts the ones. [Decimals in Context]

43. **A** If May deposits $45.50, her new balance will be ($646 − $12.25) + $45.50 = $679.25. [Decimals in Context]

44. **G** The sale price of $12.25 can be rounded down to the nearest whole number, which is $12. If this is half the price, multiply by 2 to get the regular price ($12 × 2 = $24). $25 is the closest estimate of the regular price. Option F is not as close of an estimate as $25.00. Option H divides the sale price by 2. Option J doubles the regular price instead of the sale price. [Estimation]

45. **C** The other options all equal 6. [Equivalent Form]

46. **G** 8 makes both number sentences true: 17 − 8 = 9 and 9 + 8 = 17. Option F would make the following untrue statements: 17 − 7 = 9 and 9 + 7 = 17. Option H would make these sentences untrue statements: 17 − 9 = 9 and 9 + 9 = 18. Option J incorrectly adds the numbers in each number sentence. [Properties]

47. **D** 25 light bulbs are divided by the number of light bulbs that fit in a box, 6 (25 ÷ 4 = 6 with a remainder of 1 light bulb). Option A would equal only 12 light bulbs (3 boxes with 4 light bulbs). Option B would equal only 16 light bulbs. Option C would equal only 20 light bulbs. [Divisibility]

48. **H** 14 and 23 are rounded down to 10 and 20 because the digits in the ones place are less than 5. 27 is rounded up because the number in the ones place is greater than 5. In option F, 27 is rounded down. In option G, 23 is rounded up. In option J, 14 and 23 are rounded up. [Rounding]

49. **D** The dots on the blocks increase in this pattern: + 2, + 3, + 4, + 5, so the last block will be + 6, for a total of 21 dots. Options A, B, and C do not follow this pattern. [Patterns and Shapes]

50. **H** 2 × 2 = 4, 4 − 4 = 0; 3 × 2 = 6, 6 − 4 = 2, and so on. The Output for the first box for option F would be 4. The Output for option G would be 5. The Output for option J would be 2. [Functions and Patterns]